TARSUS OR JERUSALEM
THE CITY OF PAUL'S YOUTH

TARSUS
OR
JERUSALEM
The City of Paul's Youth

BY

W. C. VAN UNNIK

TRANSLATED OUT OF THE DUTCH

BY

GEORGE OGG

LONDON
THE EPWORTH PRESS

FIRST PUBLISHED IN 1962

BS
2506
48513

PRINTED IN GREAT BRITAIN BY ROBERT MACLEHOSE AND CO. LTD
THE UNIVERSITY PRESS, GLASGOW

Contents

INTRODUCTION   *page* 1

THE PRESENT POSITION OF THE INQUIRY   5

DISCUSSION OF ACTS 22³   17

OTHER TEXTS CONNECTED WITH PAUL'S YOUTH   46

CONCLUSION AND PERSPECTIVES   52

APPENDIX I — THE USE OF τρέφω AND ITS DERIVA-
       TIVES IN CONNECTION WITH UPBRINGING   59

APPENDIX II — CHRONOLOGICAL BIBLIOGRAPHY   73

Introduction

WHAT TOOK place on the road to Damascus (Acts 9[1ff] and parallels) marks *the* big turning point in the career of the apostle Paul; from that moment onwards, the zealot for the Jewish Law was the 'slave of Jesus Christ'. In consequence, two clear-cut, separated periods in his development can be recognized: his life as a Jew and his life as a Christian. But however highly the importance of this division may be rated, for a correct insight into Paul's life and work it is desirable to take into account not two, but three periods. This becomes evident from his own autobiographical notes and from the reports in the book of the Acts when these are closely examined. There is, however, no express statement, and the matter remains in some obscurity since neither Paul nor Luke set out to furnish a biography.

There is still much uncertainty about the chronological determination of these periods.[1] For the purpose of this study it is not necessary to venture upon an attempt to clear this up or to add yet another to the already numerous calculations. A very general, rough outline is all that is needed; but, as will appear from what follows, it is indispensable. We make then these divisions:

(1) The period of Paul's youth, during which he studied and walked in the Jewish religion and which closed with his conversion. For lack of data the duration of this period of his life cannot be determined.

(2) His first years as a Christian, which he spent partly in Arabia and partly in Tarsus (Cilicia). About these years little is

---

[1] See, e.g., the table in D. Plooij, *De chronologie van het leven van Paulus* (Leiden, 1919), between pages 173 and 175; J. de Zwaan, *Inleiding tot het Nieuwe Testament* (2nd edn, Haarlem, 1948), pp. xi–xii; P. Feine–J. Behm, *Einleitung in das Neue Testament* (9th edn, Heidelberg, 1950), pp. 125–8.

known, for Luke makes no mention at all of the stay in Arabia;
and although he mentions the Cilician episode, he leaves us in
uncertainty as to how many years elapsed between what is
reported in Acts 9^{30} and what is reported in 11^{25}. In Galatians
1$^{17-18}$ Paul himself reports that his stay in Arabia was of three
years duration, and that thereafter, with a short break of
fifteen days in Jerusalem, he went to Syria and Cilicia, where
he preached the Gospel, and then returned to Jerusalem after
fourteen years (Gal 1^{21}–2^1). In this little piece of autobio-
graphy with its apologetic purpose, has he also in view that
activity of his which is reported in Acts 13? Without going
closely into this ticklish question,[1] we can certainly say that
what is spoken of here is a fairly long period, assuredly one of
at least ten years. About it nothing further is known to us,
save that throughout the whole of it Paul the Christian lived
and preached in the vicinity of Damascus and in the regions
about Tarsus and Antioch. Lack of data makes this portion
of time appear as a mere incident in Paul's biography, but
because of its duration it cannot possibly be considered unimportant.

(3) The last period is that which Luke introduces with this
special instruction of the Holy Spirit: 'Set apart for me Barna-
bas and Saul for the work to which I have called them' (Acts
13^2).[2] This is the time within which Paul did his work of
world-wide historical and theological importance. Within this
period, which runs on to his death, fall his great journeys
through Asia Minor and Greece, to Rome and perhaps to
Spain; it is from these years that his epistles date; and it is to
them that the information given in Acts almost exclusively
refers. This last and most important portion of Paul's life comprises approximately eighteen years; and it is about the mature

---

[1] On this see the various 'Introductions' to the New Testament and
commentaries on the Epistle to the Galatians.
[2] These words with which Luke particularly underlines the beginning of this period are quoted here because they are so striking. Paul
does not himself speak of this happening. We do not wish, in mention-
ing this, to make any decision in the matter of the question referred
to in the foregoing note.

man of these years that we speak when we discuss 'Paul' — a fact which we ought always to keep in view.

One part of the bulky complex of questions which Paul's biography sets us will here be submitted to a closer investigation, the question namely of the years of his youth, in particular the question whether he spent these years in Tarsus or in Jerusalem.

Although we shall come back to it in greater detail at the close of our study, the significance of this subject may for the present be indicated by the following considerations. Modern psychology has disclosed what a great role the environment and impressions of our youth, even of our very earliest years, play in the further development of our personality and in the shaping of our attitude towards our fellows and the outside world. Indeed it is superfluous to enlarge on this. Just here, where the data for the development of the apostle are very scanty, we must consider with special care the few points which appear to afford us some standing-ground.

Something more ought to be said about the specific environment indicated in our subject. In itself it may be worth while to ascertain where he, who later says of himself (I Cor 9[19ff]) that to the Jews he has become a Jew and to the Greeks a Greek, acquired the first imprints of his multi-coloured life. Although the Roman rule imparted a certain measure of uniformity, there was nevertheless a perceptible difference in scope and mentality between places such as Rome and Athens, Alexandria and Corinth, Antioch and Tarsus, to name only a few centres of culture and to make no comparisons with small provincial towns and villages or with the countryside. But the question — Tarsus or Jerusalem? — confronts us not with a distinction in degree, a demographic or cultural distinction, but with one of a very specific kind; between the two names there yawned a wide and deep cleft. Tarsus was a typically Hellenistic city, favourably situated for trade and commerce, the intellectual centre of a flourishing Stoic school, from the religious point of view an instance of syncretism in its many-coloured variations. Almost fifty years ago, in a study that is still very valuable,

Böhlig, not the first writer on the subject, but the most complete, delineated the intellectual life of this city so that it stands out clear before us.[1] Judaism, which was distinguished from all other religions principally by its monotheism,[2] was indeed represented there, but only by a minority. Let us set by the side of this the picture of Jerusalem as it has been described, for example, by Joachim Jeremias.[3] It was a place unfavourably situated for trade, but was the mother-city of Judaism, to which the heart of every Jew in the Diaspora went out; syncretism secured no footing there and Hellenistic culture could force a way in only with difficulty and only very superficially; it was dominated by the temple of Jehovah, the only God, and its life was decisively defined by the law of Moses and its interpretation. Here one religion embraced the whole of life. In these two cities, two worlds stand over against one another, radically different, each with its own questions and its own stamp, with its own attitude to life and its own aims. No more need be said to make it clear that according as a life was fashioned in the one environment or the other, its development must have been different.

As has been said, we have at our disposal only a few reports about Paul's youth, and these will be closely discussed in the course of the argument. This scanty information affords investigators much room for the play of fancy, but needs to be interpreted with extreme caution. As will appear, plentiful use has so far been made of the former; but the latter, which ought to have precedence, has in my opinion been lacking.

[1] H. Böhlig, *Die Geisteskultur von Tarsos im augusteischen Zeitalter* (Göttingen, 1913).

[2] See my contribution, 'Het *Jodendom in de verstrooiing*', in J. H. Waszink–W. C. van Unnik–Ch. de Beus, *Het oudste Christendom en de antieke cultuur* (Haarlem, 1951), Pt. I, pp. 544 ff.

[3] J. J. Jeremias, *Jerusalem zur Zeit Jesu* (2nd edn, Berlin, 1958); see also the well-known works of Schürer, Bousset–Gressmann, Moore, and the contribution of P. A. H. de Boer to *Het oudste Christendom en de antieke cultuur*, Pt. I.

The Present Position of the Inquiry

THE READER who has to some extent, even if it be super-ficially, acquainted himself with modern Pauline research, in so far as it has referred to the question here put down for discussion,[1] will perhaps be inclined to ask whether the decision about it has not been given long since. There is indeed no other point that one can mention about which, among scholars of divergent confessions and schools, such unanimity prevails as the one now before us. With few exceptions, all commentators and biographers, writers of articles in encyclo-pedias and of monographs, prefer Tarsus.[2] This preference finds very characteristic expression in the 'Symposium' which was published in 1951 on the occasion of the Greek com-memoration of Paul. In it three very different writers give their opinion upon our subject, and each of them allows Paul to spend his youth in Tarsus in order that his removal to Jerusa-lem may be put later.[3] Similarly, A. Oepke, in a well-known study in which he deals with the *Probleme der vorchristlichen Zeit des Paulus*,[4] passes by our subject in complete silence, apparently seeing in it no problem at all.

[1] Since it is in the third period that we know Paul most of all, it is understandable that very many writings are especially occupied with it and do not treat of his youth.

[2] In Appendix II, pp. 73–6, there is listed in chronological order a number of references to modern literature. It has seemed to me better, for technical reasons, to place these in a separate addendum. Naturally the list is not complete, but it is, I believe, sufficiently representative to let it be seen that here we can speak of a *communis opinio*.

[3] See *Paulus-Hellas-Oikumene (an ecumenical Symposium)*, published by the Student Christian Association of Greece (Athens, 1951): pp. 9–21, K. Adam, '*Der junge Paulus*'; W. H. P. Hatch, p. 93; W. F. Howard, p. 97.

[4] Article in *Theologische Studien und Kritiken*, CV.(1933).387–424. J. Dupont, *Les Problèmes du livre des Actes d'après les travaux récents* (Louvain, 1950), is also silent on this subject.

Our most detailed piece of information about Paul's youth is
what we read in Acts 22³. [1] This text, supplemented with a
few other data from the Acts [2] and from Paul himself (Philippians 3⁵ and the impression made upon us by his epistles with
their peculiar mixture of Jewish and Greek elements), serves as
basis for the description of his youth. Now Tarsus and
Jerusalem are mentioned here, and these names serve as incen-
tives to conjure up a picture. Thanks to the information which
is at our disposal about life in these two towns, one may
sketch, in outline or in some detail according to the available
space, a picture of his development. Its course can be summarized as follows. He was born as a Jewish child in Tarsus
where his father possessed the rights of a citizen, and he himself was also able to be proud of the fact that he was a *civis
Romanus*. His family was rigorously legalistic-Jewish, and associated itself with the Pharisees. At home and in the synagogue
of the diaspora-congregation he received his earliest instruction
in the ancestral worship and also learned the speech of his
people. At the same time, however, as he roamed on the streets
and by the harbour, he got to know in his 'most impressionable
years' [3] the life of his Hellenistic native town. As a spiritual
heritage from Tarsus he bore with him into his later life his
easy mastery of the Greek tongue, his use of the Septuagint,
and his whole manner of life — which cannot be called
genuinely Jewish. [4] After sketching this heathen environment
one passes on to a description of life in Jerusalem, since Paul

---

[1] It is not necessary in the context of this study to consider the
correctness of the tradition which appears in Hieronymus and for
which especially Th. Zahn (*Einleitung in das Neue Testament* [3rd edn,
Leipzig, 1906], I.48–50) has pleaded, that Paul's family originated
from Gischala in Galilee.

[2] These will be discussed more closely in the course of the present
study, pp. 46–51.

[3] T. Wilson, *St Paul and Paganism* (Edinburgh, 1927), p. 40: 'The
environment in which a man spends the most impressionable years of
his life leaves an indelible mark upon his character. It is therefore
highly important that we should get a true estimate of the influence of
Tarsus in the making of St Paul'; cf. a similar statement, ibid., p. 29.

[4] This is summed up briefly by Böhlig, *Die Geisteskultur von Tarsos*,
pp. 142–52. It is also instructive, with the help of the index, to go
through the passages in Wilson, loc. cit., in which the influence of

also studied there under the celebrated jurist Gamaliel. This transition took place at a time of life 'which we are left to conjecture', [1] but the great journey far from the parental home took place according to general conviction — even when there is no attempt to date it with close precision — at a time when Paul had already cast off childish ways and had given evidence of the excellent talent which seemed to foreordain him with his fervid nature for the rabbinate. When guesses are ventured, the datings run all the way from Paul's 8th to his 10th year (Zahn) on to his 13th year (Prat) and even to his 15th (Holzner, van Imschoot, Loewenich, Adam). [2] But whatever his exact age, it is generally agreed that Paul, a Jew of the Diaspora, was at this time, to put it in Klausner's words, 'grown up' but 'still in the springtime of life'.

In this manner Karl Adam has recently sketched a gloomy picture of Paul's youth, in which all sorts of general utterances in the epistles are interpreted as the outcome of experiences which he had in his parental home and at school. Did not this development provide an excellent preparation for him who was to be called to preach in the Hellenistic world the Gospel of Jesus Christ, the fulfilment of the Old Testament? Does it not present us with an explanation of the peculiar blending in him of all sorts of elements of Jewish and Hellenistic origin? The influences upon him of Hellenistic culture and of contact with heathen religious life were restrained for a time by rabbinical training, but after his conversion, when he knew that he had been called to be an apostle to the Gentiles, they burst forth with mighty power.

I will reproduce briefly the prevailing opinion in three quotations from investigators belonging to very different schools. Steinmann introduces his monograph on our subject with these words: 'I have entitled my exposition "*Zum Werde-gang des Paulus*" because I hold that Paul's native place, his

Tarsus is mooted. We may also compare J. Klausner, *From Jesus to Paul* (London, 1946), *passim*, in which Paul is delineated and explained as a typical Jew of the Diaspora.

[1] T. R. Glover, *Paul of Tarsus* (4th edn, London, 1938), p. 15.

[2] For these references see Appendix II, pp. 73–6.

home and the period of his youth had a fundamental and en-
during influence on his development. These three factors are
all found in Tarsus.'[1] In his résumé Bultmann writes: Paul
'was born and grew up in Tarsus in Cilicia', whereas he
considers the stay in Jerusalem even very doubtful;[2] and
the excellent English New Testament scholar W. F. Howard
says: Paul 'was a Jew of the Diaspora, born and brought up in
Tarsus, the chief city of the province of Cilicia, who had the
advantage of being trained in the Jewish law in the school of
the famous rabbi Gamaliel in Jerusalem'.[3]

Tarsus thus came first, being the town of Paul's youth;
Jerusalem came second, when he was somewhat older and of
an age at which his mind was already formed. As interesting
extra-biblical parallels to this order of things, as it is usually
visualized, one may point to the journey which princes of the
dynasty of Adiabene, who had gone over to Judaism, under-
took to Jerusalem that there they might be instructed more
fully,[4] and to the story of the rabbi Hillel.[5]

[1] *Zum Werdegang des Paulus, die Jugendzeit in Tarsus* (Freiburg i.
Br., 1928), p. 4. This book of thirty-nine pages is wholly built up on
this theme.

[2] R. Bultmann, '*Paulus*', in *Die Religion in Geschichte und Gegenwart*
(2nd edn, Tübingen, 1930), Vol. IV, cols. 1020–1.

[3] W. F. Howard, *Paulus-Hellas-Oikumene*, p. 97. Cf. Böhlig, *Die
Geisteskultur von Tarsos*, p. 153: 'As everything goes to prove that
Paul acquired the fundamentals of his education and intellectual
culture in Tarsus, so his epistles from beginning to end bear upon
them the stamp of the Judaism of the Dispersion'; also A. E. J.
Rawlinson, *The New Testament Doctrine of Christ* (London, 1926),
pp. 85–6: 'St Paul was a bilingual Jew from the Greek-speaking city of
Tarsus in Cilicia — a Jew who, despite the fact that he had been *born
and brought up* in the Diaspora was able to speak not only Greek, but
Aramaic; . . . the youthful Saul, after having received in boyhood,
perhaps from a Jewish *rhetor* of Hellenistic education a sufficient
training in grammar and rhetoric . . . was sent to complete his studies
at Jerusalem' [italics mine].

[4] Josephus, *Ant. Jud.*, XX.3–4.§71: 'and having besides sent his
sons, five in number, and they but young also, to learn accurately
the language of our nation, together with our learning' (trans. Whiston,
n. edn, Margoliouth).

[5] H. L. Strack, 'Hillel', in *Realencyclopädie für protestantische
Theologie und Kirche* (3rd edn, Leipzig, 1900), p. 74; according to
tradition he came when forty years of age from Babylon to Jerusalem
to study there.

That something is wrong with this interpretation of Acts 22[3] has been indicated in a remark of Deissmann, a pioneer in the field of New Testament Greek, and more recently by Dibelius–Kümmel. [1] With reference to the phrase 'brought up' (ἀνατεθραμμένος) they remark that it sounds as if Paul had already come to Jerusalem as a small child; 'but in view of the Hellenistic elements in his thought that would be an improbable assertion' (Dibelius). This difficulty is got round by interpreting 'brought up' with Deissmann as 'thoroughly instructed in the law', [2] or by assuming with Walter Bauer [3] two nuances in ἀνατρέφω, namely a physical and an intellectual culture, or by defining with Grosheide [4] the difference between the two verbs in 22[3b] thus: the first refers to the physical, the second to the intellectual upbringing. Puukko, who relates in detail what Paul would learn as a Jew in the synagogue of his

[1] A. Deissmann, *Paulus* (2nd edn, Tübingen, 1925), p. 71: 'That may best be taken to mean that Paul came to Jerusalem when still a small child. But to judge from the total impression which the Paul whom we know makes upon us, it is assuredly likely that this son of Tarsus spent his boyhood in his Hellenistic native town.' Cf. also p. 74, note 10. — M. Dibelius–W. G. Kümmel, *Paulus* (Berlin, 1951), p. 30; cf. also p. 28.

[2] R. J. Knowling ('The Acts of the Apostles', in *The Expositor's Greek Testament*, II.456–7) takes ἀνατεθραμμένος as 'educated' and refers us to 4 Maccabees 10[2] and 11[15]. 'Probably', he writes, 'Paul went to Jerusalem not later than thirteen, possibly at eleven, for his training as a teacher of the law.'

[3] W. Bauer, *Griechisch-deutsches Wörterbuch zu den Schriften des Neuen Testaments und der übrigen urchristlichen Literatur* (5th edn, Berlin, 1958), col. 127, s. v. Very curious is the position of M. Goguel in M. Goguel–H. Monnier, *Le Nouveau Testament* (Paris, 1929), p. 229: 'Paul was brought up in Jerusalem. . . . The Greek word means literally *nurtured*. Accordingly it may indicate that the apostle received all his primary education in the Holy City. But doubtless the sense of the word ought not (*il ne faut pas*) to be pressed so far; and the thought is permissible that in Tarsus Paul acquired not only his knowledge of Greek but also his Hellenistic culture.' He knows the exact meaning of the word, but tones it down to safeguard Paul's education in Tarsus. He does not give any philological reason for this treatment of the text, except his own assurance, '*il ne faut pas*', etc., and that can hardly be called good evidence.

[4] F. W. Grosheide, *De Handelingen der Apostelen* (Amsterdam, 1948), Pt. II, p. 284, note 1. So also K. Lake–H. J. Cadbury in their commentary, *The Beginnings of Christianity*, *The Acts of the Apostles*, IV.(London, 1933).278.

native town and what in addition to that he would receive at
college in Jerusalem, says that it is not clear how long he
studied under Gamaliel, but that ἀνατεθραμμένος 'is evidence
of a longer stay'. [1] But although these statements are made, it is
nevertheless the general opinion already outlined that is
arrived at.

A similar line is taken by E. Jacquier. [2] He considers first
the interpretation of ἀνατεθραμμένος = nurtured (Acts 7^{20},
Lk 4^{16}) and says: 'That is the obvious meaning; the word then
stands clearly over against πεπαιδευμένος which has Paul's
intellectual education in view. . . . If this meaning is accepted,
Paul must have come to Jerusalem when little more than an
infant.' But Jacquier prefers to take the verb in the derived
sense 'to fashion the mind' (4 Mac 10^2, 11^{15}) because 'Paul
apparently intended the term in this sense, for it was of little
importance to the Jews to know that he had been nurtured in
Jerusalem, whereas it gratified them that he had been brought
up at the feet of Gamaliel, that there his understanding had
been moulded and that as a result he had been imbued with his
teaching'. It remains to be seen whether this interpretation is
valid in view of the philological facts (see below, Appendix I)
and whether what Paul had done before his rabbinical training
under Gamaliel was unimportant to the Jews (see p. 47).

The general opinion referred to above is so current among
New Testament scholars that one such as my predecessor
A. M. Brouwer, [3] who is always ready to discuss the diverse
standpoints on a specific question, mentions no disagreement
on this matter. It should nevertheless not be left unnoticed
that disagreement does exist, although only among individuals
and without exercising any influence. Without giving names,
Böhlig mentions the old opinion that Paul 'was moved to
Jerusalem when only a child'; he thinks, however, that the
objections to this are insurmountable. According to him,

[1] A. F. Puukko, 'Paulus und das Judentum', in Studia Orientalia
Fennica, II.(Helsinki, 1928).10 ff; the passage cited is on p. 23.

[2] E. Jacquier, Les Actes des Apôtres (Paris, 1926), loc. cit.

[3] Paulus de Apostel (Zutphen, 1934), Pt. II, 'De Mensch en zijn tijd',
pp. 115 ff.

ἀνατεθραμμένος is given further explanation in the words 'at the feet of Gamaliel'; Paul wanted especially to underline the fact that he had received a rabbinic education, and one was a scholar of the rabbis not when a child, but when a young man. [1] The English commentator Rackham, however, will have no such blending. In our text he distinguishes stages that are clearly different, but with this exegesis he does not combine any specific conclusions. [2] Very outspoken, also, was the French Protestant scholar A. Sabatier. He gave as the translation of ἀνατεθραμμένος 'nurtured and brought up from his most tender infancy', and added in a footnote: Paul 'was not only instructed (πεπαιδευμένος) but also nurtured and brought up from his most tender infancy in Jerusalem (ἀνατεθραμμένος). All the conjectures that have been ventured regarding a Greek education of Paul should then disappear'. [3] This was a very definite and assured opinion. But the history of New Testament scholarship shows that in this point there has been no inclination to follow Sabatier. My fellow-countryman J. Keulers may perhaps be named here also. In a popular exposition he explains ἀνατεθραμμένος as indicating 'that Paul had already come to Jerusalem as a young lad', and he points to Luke 4[16], but without giving any further indication of Paul's age or of his own position over against the prevailing opinion. [4]

A. Loisy did not discuss the text, but, as appears from his translation, he preferred Jerusalem: 'I am a Jew, born in Tarsus of Cilicia but brought up in this city — Jerusalem — educated at the feet of Gamaliel in the strictness of the law.' This, however, he regarded as a false statement introduced by the redactor of Acts. [5]

[1] Die Geisteskultur von Tarsos, p. 151.

[2] R. B. Rackham, The Acts of the Apostles (14th edn), in Westminster Commentaries (London, 1951), p. 423.

[3] A. Sabatier, L'apôtre Paul (Paris, 1912), p. 31 and note 1.

[4] De Handelingen der Apostelen, in de Boeken van het Nieuwe Testament (2nd edn, Roermond–Maaseik, 1952), Pt. IV, p. 362.

[5] A. Loisy, Les Actes des Apôtres (Paris, 1930), p. 813. A similar translation without commentary in O. Dibelius, Die werdende Kirche (5th edn, Hamburg, 1953), p. 292: 'I am a Jew born in Tarsus in Cilicia. Here in this city I spent the years of my youth. I sat at the feet of Gamaliel and carefully studied the ancestral law.'

The keenest opposition to the prevailing opinion is found, however, in what we read in Paul Feine's great study of Paul and in Norden's *Die antike Kunstprosa*. The former absolutely rejects any watered-down meaning of 'brought up', but does so without furnishing any philological proof of the correctness of his own exegesis as against the one that is current. Further, referring to Acts 26[4-5], he maintains that Paul was already in Jerusalem 'in his childhood' before he received rabbinic tuition. For that reason he declares that all accounts of impressions made on the receptive boyish mind of Paul by a Hellenistic environment are without foundation.[1]

Very remarkable is the opinion of the great and influential classical scholar Eduard Norden. In his important work, *Die antike Kunstprosa*, he also deals with Paul. He strongly protests against the method of interpreting the apostle by means of Greek rhetors and philosophers, and in this connection he says, 'To the vain arguments there belongs the fertile appeal to Tarsus. . . . "Tarsus" has on the whole for centuries been the slogan that has continually been thrown into the scales'; but he rejects this, the first of his arguments being Acts 22[3].[2] Although some scholars have maintained that this passage is not true to facts, Norden inclines to accept the information which

---

[1] *Der Apostel Paulus* (Gütersloh, 1927), pp. 416–20. It is curious that here Feine has selected as the target of his attack J. Gresham Machen's *The Origin of Paul's Religion* (London, 1921), p. 53, for when we read through that page we see how cautiously Machen has expressed himself: The words of Acts 22[3] 'might seem to suggest that Paul went to Jerusalem in early childhood, in which case his birthplace would be of comparatively little importance in his preparation for his lifework, and all the elaborate investigations of Tarsus, so far as they are intended to shed light upon the environment of the apostle in his formation years, would become valueless. But the Greek word "brought up" or "nourished" might be used figuratively in a somewhat flexible way'. Machen thus leaves the matter open and has not reached a conclusion, since he omits a linguistic investigation of the meaning of the critical word. It is not clear to me why Feine has opposed precisely one who leaves the matter in such suspense; among German New Testament scholars he could have found, in sufficient number, supporters of the opinion which according to him is wrong.

[2] His translation is: 'Born in Tarsus, *nurtured in Jerusalem, educated at the feet of Gamaliel according to the strictness of the ancestral law*' (spaced by Norden).

it conveys on the ground that it contains certain details which could not have been invented. [1] The curious thing is that his judgement is never cited in references to Paul's youth. Has this book of his gone unnoticed by theologians to whom the author of *Agnostos Theos* [2] is by no means unknown? It is a pity that Norden merely states his interpretation of Acts 22³ and does not refute the opposite opinion by exegetical arguments.

Success has not in any form attended the attempt to combat the prevailing opinion. It seems indeed that the triumphant exclamation of Steinmann, 'if at least Feine would account for Paul's absolute mastery of the Septuagint and of Greek', [3] contains a refutation that is in every respect decisive. It is only in a few cases, especially in commentaries, that we find a measure of uncertainty, and nowhere are we given a clear presentation of the opinion held by the writer concerned. [4] Of

---

[1] *Die antike Kunstprosa* (5th edn, Stuttgart, 1958), II.492 ff; the quotation is from p. 495 and note 3; he continues: 'That Paul came to Jerusalem in his youth is indeed not at all extraordinary: there was in the synagogue there a company "of people from Cilicia", Acts 6⁹' (pp. 495–6). (This 5th edition is a reprint of the 2nd edition of 1909.)

[2] Pubd Leipzig, 1913, and which had a great influence, especially on Form-criticism.

[3] Steinmann, *Zum Werdegang des Paulus*, p. 30, note 1.

[4] The opinion of J. M. S. Baljon is *not clear*. In his *Commentaar op de Handelingen der Apostelen* (Utrecht, 1903; p. 246) he writes (without any further elucidation or elaboration): 'Although born in Tarsus, he grew up in Jerusalem and was brought up as a strict Jew'; but cf. his *Geschiedenis van de boeken des Nieuwen Verbonds* (Groningen, 1901; pp. 2–3), where the 'generally accepted' opinion is found. The same is true of the opinion of P. G. Kunst, *Joodsche invloeden bij Paulus* (Amsterdam, 1936), (diss. Free University), pp. 124–5; of J. Leipoldt, *Jesus und Paulus, Paulus oder Jesus* (Leipzig, 1936; p. 12): 'It is not known up to what year of his life Paul remained in Tarsus. Was he there only as an infant? Or did he obtain there impressions from the Hellenistic world that proved important for his later life?'; see also pp. 29–30; of H. W. Beyer, *Die Apostelgeschichte* (4th edn), in *das Neue Testament Deutsch* (Göttingen, 1947), (on Acts 22³ nothing is said about this matter, but on p. 149 on Acts 26⁵ he writes: 'It was in Jerusalem itself that he received the decisive impressions of youth'); of F. W. Grosheide, *De Handelingen der Apostelen* (p. 283: 'thus young he came there' [i.e. to Jerusalem] and p. 363: 'elsewhere we also get the impression that Paul came to Jerusalem at a fairly youthful age and remained there [Acts 22³]. An age cannot be given, but it was

the vast majority of the investigators — and here we have also in mind the most recent publications — it may be said that without any doubt they are of the opinion that the apostle spent the years of his youth in the parental home at Tarsus and that this Hellenistic-syncretistic environment gave to his life an indelible stamp.

It seems to me important to study this problem afresh, especially in view of the fact that, as is quite clear from the foregoing summary, the big question of Paul's attitude to Hellenism and to his life's task as 'the apostle of the Gentiles' is thought to be closely bound up with it. It is true that an impressive phalanx of New Testament scholars, whose number suggests that we might speak of certainty on this point, has declared itself for Tarsus, but it cannot be denied that some are in doubt. For this doubt there is, I think, good reason, when what follows is taken into consideration. In the last resort the whole construction rests upon one single text, which contains the only definite data about the years of Paul's youth, namely Acts 22[3]; for it is not clear that the rest (the Hellenistic elements in Paul's epistles) ought to be explained, without more ado, by reference to the city of his birth: that is nowhere stated in the

nevertheless such that the apostle does not count or hardly counts in what befell before his coming to Jerusalem and testifies that his life was spent in the capital city'; but at Acts 26[5] one may think of Cilicia [cf. p. 47 below, and on the distinction which Grosheide makes between ἀνατεθραμμένος and πεπαιδευμένος see p. 9 above]); of A. D. Nock, St Paul (London, 1946), (p. 33: 'Probably Paul had been at Jerusalem, as man if not as boy'; but the whole tendency of his second chapter [pp. 21–34] is of such a character that the influence of Tarsus is assumed, and for this reason we enter Nock's name in Appendix II). On Bauerfeind, see p. 30 below. The question is *not discussed* in the commentaries of E. Preuschen, *Die Apostelgeschichte* (Tübingen, 1912); G. Hoennicke, *Die Apostelgeschichte* (Leipzig, 1913); H. H. Wendt, *Die Apostelgeschichte* (Göttingen, 1913); R. Knopf, 'Apostelgeschichte', in *Die Schriften des Neuen Testaments* (3rd edn, Göttingen, 1917), Vol. III; Lake–Cadbury, *The Beginnings of Christianity, The Acts of the Apostles* (although they decide for 'Cilicia' in Acts 26[5] — see p. 47 below); H. J. Holtzmann, *Die Apostelgeschichte* (3rd edn, Tübingen–Leipzig, 1901); A. W. F. Blunt, *Acts of the Apostles* (Oxford, 1923), (Clarendon Bible); or A. Boudon, *Actes des Apôtres* (6th edn, Paris, 1933), p. 486.

New Testament and is but a hypothesis. Now in reading Acts 22³ we are faced with the fact that in the beginning of the verse nothing more is said than that Paul was *born* in Tarsus; yet according to Steinmann, Bultmann, and Howard, whom we have cited as clear exponents of the '*communis opinio*', we read that he was *born and grew up* there. The question is: where have the words 'and grew up' come from; are they smuggled in to prove the case? An answer to this question, a question which never seems to be thought worth the trouble of putting, but which is nevertheless of decisive significance, is sorely lacking. But therewith the whole matter remains unsettled.

To this a second question which prompts us to make renewed investigation ought to be added. In the generally accepted sketch of Paul's youth he is first for a number of years in Tarsus, and thereafter in Jerusalem that he may study under Gamaliel. That explains the words 'born' ($\gamma\epsilon\gamma\epsilon\nu\nu\eta\mu\acute{\epsilon}\nu o\varsigma$) and 'instructed' ($\pi\epsilon\pi\alpha\iota\delta\epsilon\upsilon\mu\acute{\epsilon}\nu o\varsigma$) in Acts 22³, but what does one do with 'brought up' ($\dot{\alpha}\nu\alpha\tau\epsilon\theta\rho\alpha\mu\mu\acute{\epsilon}\nu o\varsigma$) that stands between them? Even though most translations of this passage give quite correctly two verbs, it appears from discussions of it that 'brought up ... instructed' is almost universally understood as a hendiadys — hence a rendering such as the one given with no beating about the bush by Oort: 'I am a Jew born at Tarsus in Cilicia, but brought up in this town at the feet of Gamaliel according to the strict requirements of the ancestral law.'[1] But is this quite correct? It is most singular that very many authors do not touch upon this question with a single word and that others who certainly mention it — and this holds good of supporters and opponents of the current view — never give an accurate philological analysis of the notion $\dot{\alpha}\nu\alpha\tau\rho\acute{\epsilon}\phi\omega$ and the interpretation of this verse that results from it. The observations which we meet with scattered here and there are never supported by texts (cf. p. 9 and pp. 29–30).

This is, then, a peculiar and unsatisfactory situation: on the one hand certain words (and therewith a very significant

[1] *Het Nieuwe Testament opnieuw uit den grondtekst vertaald* (Zaltbommel, 1912), p. 285.

thought) are added to the text without reasons being given; on the other hand a word which stands there is left practically unexplained. Renewed investigation is therefore required, and it will have to examine precisely that matter in which previous investigation has failed us, namely, the accurate determination of the content of ἀνατεθραμμένος. We must be mindful of the truth of Söderblom's dictum: 'Philology is the eye of the needle through which every theological camel must enter into the heaven of divinity.'[1]

[1] Quoted in J. M. van Veen, *Nathan Söderblom* (Amsterdam, 1940), (diss. Groningen), p. 59, note 4.

Discussion of Acts 22³

ACTS 22 reproduces the defence which Paul is supposed to have made in Aramaic before the Jewish multitude. In it he tells how he, a Jew by birth and upbringing who had devoted himself completely to the religion of his fathers, had yet been brought to see the Messiah in Jesus and to preach Him. Verse 3 is an independent account of the years of his youth, and the context is of no importance for its interpretation. The text is as follows:

ἐγώ εἰμι ἀνὴρ Ἰουδαῖος, γεγεννημένος ἐν Ταρσῷ τῆς Κιλικίας, ἀνατεθραμμένος δὲ ἐν τῇ πόλει ταύτῃ παρὰ τοὺς πόδας Γαμαλιὴλ πεπαιδευμένος κατὰ ἀκρίβειαν τοῦ πατρῴου νόμου, ζηλωτὴς ὑπάρχων τοῦ θεοῦ καθὼς πάντες ὑμεῖς ἐστε σήμερον.

(1) No peculiarities calling for text-criticism present themselves here. But the question as to the correct punctuation certainly merits our attention for a moment. Should a comma be read after ἐν τῇ πόλει ταύτῃ or after παρὰ τοὺς πόδας Γαμαλιήλ? In other words, did the activity of the celebrated rabbi[1] extend over the παιδεύειν alone or did it extend over the ἀνατρέφειν as well? According to Wendt, the fact that each new participle can introduce a closer definition is in favour of the second of these views; but the fact that the sitting at the feet of Gamaliel belongs to the upbringing in the Law is material reason for the first.[2] The symmetry of the sentence requires, so Steinmann

¹ See H. L. Strack–P. Billerbeck, *Kommentar zum Neuen Testament aus Talmud und Midrasch* (München, 1924), II.636–9, and other commentaries on Acts 5³⁴.

² H. H. Wendt, *Die Apostelgeschichte*, on Acts 22³. Cf. also the edition of E. Nestle (Stuttgart, 1953), loc. cit., the text of which is cited here, but without the doubtful punctuation.

δέ has of course adversative force; οὗτος = this, see Bauer, *Griechisch-deutsches Wörterbuch zu den Schriften des Neuen Testaments*, col. 1182.

asserts, that the comma be read after 'Gamaliel'; that, he admits, certainly seems to be a trifle, but, so he continues, to read it after ταύτῃ is to be guilty of 'an exegetical misunderstanding', for then it would have to be gathered from the text that Paul had already come to Jerusalem as a little child, and that is impossible. [1] At the present time the comma is usually read after 'this city', but according to Lake–Cadbury it can be said (to the relief of Steinmann?) that it does not make much difference, for although ἀνατρέφω usually refers to physical care, it can also be used of 'education' like παιδεύω. [2] If then the first of the above-mentioned views is preferred, as hitherto it generally has been, [3] the text says nothing other than that the apostle was born in Tarsus and was trained in Jerusalem, and that leaves ample room to allow of his coming to the city in his fifteenth year. If the punctuation now generally adopted is adhered to, the question of what ἀνατρέφω really means becomes an urgent one. The answer to it seems to be clearly given in the words of Lake–Cadbury. But on this point a decision cannot yet be reached. From the manuscripts no 'decisive evidence' (Lake–Cadbury) can be expected, since they give no punctuation at all. Punctuation was introduced by the later editors and is thus a matter of exegesis. Consequently it is advisable to pass on to exegesis and to postpone a decision about the punctuation.

(2) We begin with an observation of a critical nature on the matter of style. In describing the first phase of Paul's development — it seems trivial to mention this expressly, but to do so appears to be necessary — Luke uses three verbs: γεγεννημένος in Tarsus, and ἀνατεθραμμένος and πεπαιδευμένος in this city (i.e. Jerusalem). [4] Steinmann wrongly assumes a fourth, for he

---

[1] *Zum Werdegang des Paulus, die Jugendzeit in Tarsus*, p. 29.

[2] Lake–Cadbury in their commentary, loc. cit.

[3] Of the publications of recent years only one has come under my notice which puts the comma after Gamaliel, namely the American *Revised Standard Version* of 1946.

[4] For a good formal parallel, reference may be made to Josephus, *Bell*, Jud., II.7.1.§101: 'In the meantime there was a man, who was by birth a Jew but brought up at Sidon with one of the Roman freedmen.'

includes ὑπάρχων in the series.[1] In doing so he overlooks the fact that the first three verbs are in the perfect whilst the last is a present participle, which means a difference in the wording that ought not to be ignored. To rely here upon the rhythm of the sentence, as he does, is somewhat hazardous; the rhythm will have to accord with the meaning of the words. Finally — and this clinches the matter — he has not kept in view the fact that Luke's wording is not an accidental concatenation of verbs.

It is a remarkable fact that up to the present in not a single discussion of this text has it been pointed out that *this triad* forms *a fixed literary unit*, in which small variations in the wording are sometimes met with. A number of instances may be given here:[2]

PLATO, *Alcib.*, I.122.B — The development of Alcibiades contrasted with that of the Persian royal children: 'But about your birth (γενέσεως), Alcibiades, or nurture (τροφῆς), or education (παιδείας), or about those of any other Athenian, one may say that nobody cares, unless it be some lover whom you chance to have.'[3]

Leg., VI.783.B — παίδων δὲ δὴ γένεσιν μετὰ τοὺς γάμους θῶμεν, καὶ μετὰ γένεσιν τροφὴν καὶ παιδείαν.

Leg., VIII.842.E — After the most important laws which treat περὶ γάμους ἅμα καὶ γενέσεις παίδων καὶ τροφάς, ἔτι δὲ καὶ παιδείας ἀρχῶν τε καταστάσεις ἐν τῇ πόλει there come the simple laws which treat of food.

Menex., 237.A — 'Wherefore let us first of all praise the goodness of their birth (εὐγένειαν); secondly, their nurture (τροφήν) and education (παιδείαν).'

Epin., 973.D — The Athenian points out how diverse human life is, but that the main processes, namely τὸ γίγνεσθαι,

---

[1] *Zum Werdegang des Paulus*, p. 29. From the instances given below it is evident that in some cases, where it appeared desirable for the story, the treble formula was amplified with terms which described life after the period of youth.

[2] It is of course not claimed that the list of instances given here is complete. The works of only a few writers have been scrutinized, but the result is amply sufficient to enable a conclusion to be built up.

[3] *Loeb Library* trans.

καὶ τὸ τρέφεσθαι ἔτι καὶ παιδεύεσθαι, bring with them difficulties for all.

Crito, 50.D — The laws ask Socrates what complaints he has against them: 'Are we not your parents? Was it not through us that your father took your mother and begat you?'; or against those of them 'that regulate the nurture (τροφήν) and education (παιδείαν) of the child (τοῦ γενομένου), which you, like others, received'. If all that is true, may you then abandon us, the laws ask, 'since you were brought into the world (ἐγένου) and nurtured (ἐξετράφης) and educated (ἐπαιδεύθης) by us'? (50.E). 51.C — The laws address Socrates and have a right to speak, 'for we brought you into the world (γεννήσαντες), we nurtured (ἐκθρέψαντες) you, we educated (παιδεύσαντες) you, we gave you a share of all the good things we could.'

Compare also *Timaeus* 23.D, where the priest of the Egyptians, speaking about the origin of their peoples, says: 'But, chiefly, for the sake of the goddess, your patron,[1] foster-mother and tutress, and ours.'

ISOCRATES, Περὶ τοῦ ζευγοῦς, ii (28) — Regarding Alcibiades, who as an orphan was brought up by Pericles: 'For I count this also among his blessings that, being of such origin (ἐκ τοιούτων γενομένον), he was fostered (ἐπιτροπευθῆναι), reared (τραφῆναι), and educated (παιδευθῆναι) under the guardianship of a man of such character.'

PHILO, *de Leg. alleg.*, I.31.§99, treats of the respect due to parents; the reason for it is ἐγέννησαν ἡμᾶς, ἔθρεψαν, ἐπαίδευσαν, πάντων αἴτιοι γεγόνασιν ἀγαθῶν.

In Flaccum, 19.§158 — Concerning Flaccus: ὁ γεννηθεὶς μὲν καὶ τραφεὶς καὶ παιδευθεὶς ἐν τῇ ἡγεμονίδι 'Ρώμῃ.

De Somniis, II.21.§147 — εἴτε δι᾽ εὐμοιρίαν φύσεως[2] εἴτε διὰ τὴν τῶν τρέφοντων καὶ παιδεύοντων ἐπιμέλειαν.

Here there may be added for purposes of comparison *In*

---

[1] H. G. Liddell–R. Scott, *A Greek-English Lexicon* (Oxford, 1940), II.1022.

[2] φύσις is here the nature, the character which we are given at birth.

Flaccum, 7.§46: The Jews consider the lands where they dwell in the Diaspora ἕκαστοι πατρίδας, ἐν αἷς ἐγεννήθησαν καὶ ἐτράφησαν: naturally the last member of the triad is omitted here, because for the Jews παιδεύω consisted in the teaching of the Law, and that of course could not be said of Gentile lands. With this there may also be compared the wording of Josephus, *Antiq.*, II.10.1.§238, concerning Moses in Egypt, 'when he was born (γεννηθείς) and brought up (τραφείς) in the foregoing manner and come to the age of maturity'; Josephus avoids παιδεύω on purpose (cf. pp. 39 f). Can Josephus, *c. Apionem*, II.25, also be mentioned here (cf. p. 42)?

Compare also pp. 36 f on Philo's *Vita Mosis*, the beginning of which is built up on this theme, and Ezechiel Tragicus, cited on p. 40.

NICOLAUS OF DAMASCUS, *Vitae Caesaris* Prooemium (quoted by F. Leo, *Die griechisch-römische Biographie nach ihrer literarischen Form* [Leipzig, 1901], p. 191): 'I give an account of his descent and of his disposition, also of his parents (γεννητάς), from whom he received from infancy the nurture (τροφήν) and education (παίδευσιν) furnished with which he became the great man that he was.' Leo adds: 'This order is then followed in detail.'

PLUTARCH, *Conv. disp.*, VIII. quaestio 7. (p. 727.B) — A Pythagorean from Etruria attempts with all sorts of proofs to show that Pythagoras originated from that land: 'And he affirmed that Pythagoras was a Tuscan, not because his father, as others have said, was one, but because he himself was born (γεγονέναι), bred (τετράφθαι), and taught (πεπαιδεῦσθαι) in Tuscany.'[1]

Quomodo adulator, 25.(p. 65.F) — To keep a strict eye on our own development is among other things a good means of withstanding the influence of flatterers, for thereby we get to know the flaws in our own life: ἅμα καὶ φύσιν καὶ τροφὴν καὶ παίδευσιν ἑαυτῶν ἀναθεωρῶμεν.

The Life of Numa, 5.(p. 63.B) — Numa does not suffer him-

[1] Goodwin's trans.

self to be made king easily: he points to Romulus, who had many adversaries: 'Yet Romulus is celebrated as a person of divine origin, as supernaturally nurtured, when an infant, and most wondrously preserved'; how much lower does he himself stand in the matter of origin: 'But as for me, I am only of mortal race (γένος) and, as you well know, my nurture (τροφή) and education (παίδευσις) boast of nothing extraordinary.' From this parallelism it is obvious that what is here referred to is the period of youth.

Comparison of Agis-Cleomenes with the Gracchi, 41.(p. 843.F) — Of those who hated the Gracchi no one dared to say that they had not had an excellent upbringing (they were brought up by Cornelia, who in antiquity was reckoned a supreme instance of the true mother)[1]: 'Of all the Romans they were the most disposed by nature to virtue (εὐφυέστατοι), and they received a most excellent upbringing (τροφῆς) and education (παιδευσέως).'

Agis and Cleomenes also were by nature richly gifted, but in their case the essentials of a right upbringing had been wanting: 'Their disposition (φύσις) appears to have been more vigorous than theirs inasmuch they did not receive a sound education (παιδείας) and were trained (ἐκτραφέντες) to manners and customs that had corrupted the elders before them.'

In the light of these passages[2] it can be shown that in its opening chapters the structure of the book *De liberis educandis*, which stands in Plutarch's name,[3] is determined by this triple schema; for there in Chapters 1–3 problems are discussed which are connected with birth, Chapters 4–7 deal with life in the home and the upbringing which is received there under the guidance of foster-mothers and 'pedagogues' (slaves, Chapter 7), and thereafter there comes as the third phase the instruc-

[1] See the dissertation of R. Boulogne (mentioned on p. 24 *infra*), p. 18, note 3.
[2] Although these texts show a remarkable resemblance to Acts 22³, not one of them is mentioned in H. Almquist, *Plutarch und das Neue Testament* (Uppsala–Copenhagen, 1940).
[3] See A. Sizoo, *De Plutarchi qui fertur de liberis educandis libello* (Amsterdam, 1918), (diss. Free University).

tion given by διδάσκαλοι. This last is introduced with these words: 'And now I come to that which is a greater matter, and of more concern than any that I have mentioned', for in making choice of good teachers we must pay attention to the fact that the root and source of καλοκαγαθία is τὸ νομίμου τυχεῖν παιδείας (Chapter 7). The agreements between this writing and Quintilian, *Instr. Orat.*, I.1–2.4, have now for a long time attracted attention. The question has often been asked whether both do not go back to a lost work of Chrysippus. The possibility of that does not seem to me to be excluded, but apart from the general schema which is common to both — for in Quintilian also this trebling is found — agreements of a literary kind are not numerous. Be this as it may, for our investigation it is important to note that, so far as the development of youth is concerned, both works have as foundation a common schema comprising the three elements to the presence of which in other writers attention has already been called.

EPICTETUS, *Dissert.*, II.22.26 — ἀλλ᾽ ἐξέτασον μὴ ταῦθ᾽ἅ οἱ ἄλλοι, εἰ ἐκ τῶν αὐτῶν γονέων καὶ ὁμοῦ ἀνατεθραμμένοι καὶ ὑπὸ τῷ αὐτῷ παιδαγωγῷ.

The translation of D. C. Hesseling (*De Kolleges van Epictetus*, [Haarlem, 1931], p. 194), 'if they were brought up together and by the self-same tutor', does not seem to me to be entirely correct; it severs the triplet of words which are bound together by the double καί, and here ὑπό is followed not by the genitive but by the dative. One may translate thus: 'If they were born of the same parents, were brought up together and under the same pedagogue.' The parallelism with the rhetorical variation of ἐκ, ὁμοῦ and ὑπό then remains preserved. Nevertheless the question cannot fail to present itself whether in fact we have here to do with the triad which we have investigated. How ought ἀνατεθραμμένοι to be understood here? Ought we to understand it literally of the work of the foster-mother or ought we to take it, as Bauer[1] does, as referring to the training of the

---

[1] W. Bauer, *Griechisch-deutsches Wörterbuch zu den Schriften des Neuen Testaments* (5th edn), col. 124.

mind? The 'pedagogue' was usually a slave and was employed
in the upbringing of the child in the home; as the writings of
Quintilian and Plutarch named above (see also p. 64, below)
testify, he was mentioned together with the foster-mother as
responsible for the direction of the child until the time when
he was entrusted to a teacher.[1] In that case this passage
of Epictetus refers to the two stages of the child's life in the
home, and the triad for which we have looked is out of the
question. In *Diss*. III.1.35, ἀνατρέφω in the expression
φύεσθαι καὶ ἀνατρέφεσθαι refers without a doubt to nothing
more than the work of the foster-mother, the general fashioning
of a certain conduct in life, a fashioning from which the
παιδεύεσθαι was of course absent in the case of the dandies
mentioned there. Accordingly we include this passage in the
series with due reserve.

PSEUDO DIONYSIUS OF HALICARNASSUS, *Τέχνη*, 6 (as quoted in
translation by A. Boulanger, *Aelius Aristide et la sophistique
dans la province d'Asie au II*ᵉ *siècle de notre ère* [Paris, 1923],
p. 318, note 1): 'Since the funeral discourse is a eulogy of the
dead, it must evidently draw from the same sources as eulogies
of the living: native land, family, nature, education, deeds'; cf.
also Boulanger, ibid., p. 319, note 1, who cites Menander,
Περὶ ἐπιδεικτικῶν, pp. 419–20, Spengel: 'Laudatory
common-place topics: race, birth, natural qualities, education,
instruction, manners, deeds.'

CLEMENT OF ALEXANDRIA, *Strom*., III.15.98.4 — τῷ γὰρ κατὰ
λόγον τεκνοποιησαμένῳ καὶ ἀναθρεψαμένῳ καὶ παιδεύσαντι ἐν
κυρίῳ.

That for Clement this was a well-known type of formula
may appear from the fact that he also applies it in connection
with the 'new birth', in *Paed*., I.12.98.2, where it is said of

---

[1] Regarding the pedagogue, see R. Boulogne, *De plaats van de
paedagogus in de Romeinse cultuur* (Groningen–Djakarta, 1951), (diss.
Utrecht); in this work, as its title indicates, special attention is paid to
the Roman culture, but the picture that is drawn is also applicable to
the Greek portion of the Empire.

Christ that 'He regenerated man by water, and made him grow (αὐξῆσαι) by His Spirit, and trained him by His word to adoption and salvation, directing him by sacred precepts'[1] (we need not be surprised that here the verb αὐξῆσαι is used, for the meaning of τρέφω was somewhat plastic, and αὐξέω also appears in such contexts).

JAMBLICHUS, *De vita Pythagorica*, 31.§.213 — 'That men made their own off-spring of no account, but begat children (γεννᾶν) rashly and by chance, in every way acting off-hand, and thereafter nurtured (τρέφειν) and educated (παιδεύειν) them most contemptuously.'

EUSEBIUS, *Historia Eccl.*, IX.10.1 — in a comparison of Maximinus Daza with his fellow-administrators 'who were in every respect his superiors, in birth, in training, in education (γένει καὶ τροφῇ καὶ παιδείᾳ), in worth, and in intelligence (ἀξιώματί τε καὶ συνέσει)'.

From the fact that the words are joined in a different way (note the transition with τε) it certainly appears that we have here to do with an established formula and that this formula has reference to the years of youth.

PIONIUS, *Vita Polycarpi*, 3: Polycarp was purchased as a slave by a devout woman; ἔστι δὲ τοῦτο (τὸ παιδάριον) τῷ γένει ἀπὸ ἀνατολῆς; of this woman it is said ἠγαλλιάσατο ἀνατρέφουσα κοσμίως καὶ παιδεύουσα τὴν ἐν Κυρίῳ παιδείαν.

GREGORY THAUMATURGUS, *Panegyric on Origen*, made when he was about to leave Caesarea in Palestine after having studied there for five years under the direction of Origen. In a ponderously rhetorical style he surveys the course of his life, which in such a wonderful way has brought him into touch with Origen, a contact which was decisive for the rest of it. He owes this guidance to a guardian angel, who, according to the word of

---

[1] *Ante-Nicene Christian Library* trans.

Scripture in Genesis 48¹⁵, was to him ὁ τρέφων με ἐκ νεότητός μου (IV.§41)[1] and of whom he says (§44): πάλαι τε καὶ νῦν ἔτι ἐκτρέφει τε καὶ παιδεύει καὶ χειραγωγεῖ and (§46) ἄνωθεν τοῦτο (namely the meeting with his master) προμηθούμενος οἶμαι ἐκ πρώτης γενέσεως καὶ ἀνατροφῆς.[2] Of most importance for our investigation is the information about his youth which now follows (Chapter V.§§48–50): 'For my earliest upbringing (ἀνατροφαί) from the time of my birth (γενέσεως) onwards was in the hand of my parents; and the manner of life in my father's house (πάτρια ἔθη) was one of error, and of a kind from which no one, I imagine, expected that we should be delivered; nor had I myself the hope of being so, boy as I was, and without understanding, and under a superstitious father. Then followed the loss of my father and my orphanhood' — he was then fourteen years old. After a digression that is without importance for our purpose, he proceeds (§56): 'It seemed good to the only one of my parents who survived to care for me — namely, my mother — that, being already under instruction (ἐκπαιδευομένους) in other branches in which boys not ignobly born and nurtured are usually trained, I should attend also a teacher of public speaking, in the hope that I too should become a public speaker.' In §58 he says: 'He came and suggested (an extension of my studies) to one of my teachers (διδασκάλων) under whose charge I had been put, with a view to instruction (ἐκπαιδεύειν) in the Roman tongue'; this teacher urged him on to the study of Roman law, cf. §62: 'for when, willingly or unwillingly, I was being well instructed (ἐξεπαιδευόμην) in these laws, etc.'

That παιδεύειν and διδάσκειν are alike is also apparent from Chapter VII.§§105–6: περὶ ἑκάστων ἐδίδασκεν. οὕτως ... ἐξεπαιδεύετο. Here then it is also clearly apparent that the ἀνατροφή was linked to the sphere of the home and had to do with the ἔθη, that the παιδεύειν was entrusted to others, and

---

[1] Divisions according to the edition of P. Koetschau, *Des Gregorios Thaumaturgos Dankrede an Origenes* (Freiburg i.B.–Leipzig, 1894). Trans. of the *Ante-Nicene Christian Library*.

[2] Cf. also Chapter II.§11: 'It is not his descent or physical training that I am about to praise.'

that Gregory also used the well-known triad in describing his youth (especially in §56).

More evidence may be found in authentic or legendary biographies from antiquity, see, e.g., Gregorius Nyssenus, *Vita Macrinae*, ed. V. Woods-Callahan, *Gregorii Nysseni opera ascetica* (Leiden, 1952), pp. 371-4, 383; also Suidas on Mani (quoted by A. Adam, *Texte zum Manichäismus* [Berlin, 1954], p. 78): 'Instructed (παιδευθείς) in all that concerned the Greeks, he favoured the school of Empedocles . . . he asserted that he had been born (γεγενῆσθαι) of a virgin and nurtured (ἀνατραφῆναι) in the mountains.'

For the purpose of the present investigation it does not seem to be necessary, seeing that this triad occurs in so many places in Greek literature, to look for parallels in Latin literature; we may, however, cite Seneca, *Benif.*, III.17.4: *apud quem non parentum qui debet, honor est, non educatoris, non praeceptorum* (in Acts 22³ the Vulgate reads *natus, nutritus, eruditus*). My colleague H. Wagenvoort has called my attention to Varro fr. 5: *educit obstetrix, educat nutrix, instituit paedagogus, docet magister*. This apparent division into four is actually a variant of the triad, for the work of the nutrix and that of the paedagogus belong together and are concerned with the same stage of the child's development. In this connection reference may be made to Plutarch, *Quomodo adolescens poetas audire debeat*, 14.(36.E). Plutarch argues there that, by the charm of their form, poems can help to make children familiar, if only slightly, with the thoughts of the philosophers, which are the highest aim of true upbringing; what children thus manage to hear from the philosophers is altogether different from what they most often learn at home, e.g. about happiness in life: the child's head is 'confusedly full of the things he is always hearing from his mother and nurse — yea, sometimes too from his father and his teacher'. This passage is also interesting for the reason that it lets us see how things went at home (cf. p. 64, below).

The occurrence (with variations) of these three notions as a

C

connected whole in such writers as Plato and Isocrates, Philo and Josephus (?), Plutarch and Clement of Alexandria, Jamblicus and Eusebius, etc., men who all ply a literary Greek, certainly shows that we have here to do with a fixed formula (*topos*). From the use of it by Clement and Eusebius, who here deviate from Luke and so are not influenced by him, we see that it is a fixed schema; sometimes it is but a short formula, and on other occasions it is elaborated as a theme. It was the proper thing to describe the development of a man's youth in this way. That this style-motif was not unknown to Luke is evident from the fact that he makes use of it in another passage, namely Acts 7^{20-2}, where, with deviations from the LXX version but with striking parallels to Philo, the history of the youth of Moses in Egypt is given according to this schema (later on, pp. 36 ff, this passage will be considered separately, for it merits a more detailed discussion). A small but not unimportant peculiarity may here be noted: in Acts 7^{22} and 22^3 the verb παιδεύω has the same meaning as it has in literary Greek, namely to 'educate', whereas in the remaining places where it occurs in the New Testament it has the same meaning as in the LXX, namely 'to chastise'.[1] Here, then, Luke obviously moves in the sphere of the literary Greek. This agrees completely with the character of his composition, which exhibits differences in small features of the kind.[2]

In the light of these facts it seems to me unlawful to break this triad[3] and to treat its two last terms as if they had really about the same meaning. On the contrary, because we are concerned here with a consciously chosen literary motif, it is likely that each of the terms has a specific nuance and registers a definite stage on life's way. If this is so, then this difference ought of course to be fully shown both in translation and in

[1] Cf. W. Bauer, *Griechisch-deutsches Wörterbuch zu den Schriften des Neuen Testaments* (5th edn), col. 1197, and W. Jentsch, *Urchristliches Erziehungsdenken* (Gütersloh, 1951), p. 142.

[2] J. de Zwaan, 'The Use of the Greek Language in Acts', in *The Beginnings of Christianity* (London, 1922), II.30 ff.

[3] As, e.g., in the translation of H. Menge, and in that of H. W. Beyer, *Die Apostelgeschichte*, p. 134.

interpretation. No one will dispute that 'birth' is a special moment on life's way. That it is implied in this word, as is assumed over and over again in discussions of Acts 22³ (see p. 8 above), that it also relates to the years of youth, seems, in view of the texts that have been quoted, extraordinarily unlikely. But what is needed before everything else is a careful investigation of the difference between ἀνατρέφω and παιδεύω.

(3) This subject brings us on to the much neglected domain of New Testament synonyms. Fully thirty years ago F. Torm was obliged to complain that in this domain little had been done since the end of last century, and since then there has been no turn for the better.[1] In the older literature the pair of words here in question is not discussed. The more modern commentators, too, say practically nothing about it. A difference is registered, e.g. in Lake–Cadbury and Grosheide (cf. p. 9 above), but for an elucidation of it we seek in vain. Zahn has rightly objected that the difference between the two words should not be disregarded,[2] but he too sheds no light upon it from the Greek usage. Instead he manages to account for it by making a connection with Acts 23¹⁰⁻¹². Paul must have had his home for a time with his older sister who dwelt in Jerusalem, and she must have charged herself with his 'bringing up' after his eighth year (ἀνατεθραμμένος), after which there followed his training under Gamaliel to be a man learned in the law (πεπαιδευμένος). The insurmountable objection to this whole construction of Zahn is that what is reported in Acts 23 took place at a much later time, namely after the great missionary journeys; all that Zahn relates about his sister is pure phantasy, for there is not a word in Acts to say that she was older than Paul or that her brother had stayed with her. If we were unable to discover anything about ἀνατρέφω with the help of Greek texts, we might perhaps take refuge in such a hypothetical explanation, but at present it is nothing more than idle talk.

[1] *Hermeneutik des Neuen Testaments* (Göttingen, 1930), pp. 90–1.
[2] *Die Apostelgeschichte des Lukas* (1st and 2nd edns, Leipzig-Erlangen, 1921), II.751.

In what follows, the text, Acts 23[16 ff], will demand our attention, but at this point nothing is to be expected from it. The position of Bauernfeind is remarkable, not so much in the difference which he sees between the two words — 'πεπαιδευ-μένος certainly refers to the actual study of the law, whilst ἀνατεθραμμένος will include the period of babyhood' (where, without philological proof, we have to put up with the uncertain 'will') — as in the manner in which he continues: 'Both the outposts of Judaism in the Diaspora and its citadel in Jerusalem were able to exercise their *full* influence on Paul.'[(1)] In my opinion this continuation is rather unexpected and odd, especially if full weight is given to the word which I have put in italics; for if ἀνατεθραμμένος actually comprises the earliest years of childhood, it is inconceivable how Tarsus can have had such an influence that it can be called 'full'. Either the first or the second of Bauernfeind's statements must be incorrect, and meanwhile we are just as wise as we were. When finally we turn for philological help to Walter Bauer's *Wörterbuch*,[(2)] we find in it a distinction between 'physical nurture = to bring up, to care for' and 'mental and spiritual nurture = to educate', and under the latter meaning Acts 22[3] is cited. We observe, however, that according to Bauer ἀνατρέφω has the first of these shades of meaning in Acts 7[20] and the second in Acts 7[21], a verse which belongs to the same passage; and when we ask ourselves whether this is quite correct, we see that a closer investigation of the Greek texts is absolutely necessary before we can decide. Moreover, the recent work of Jentsch on '*Urchristliches Erziehungsdenken*' gives no further help in this respect, for it appears to concentrate wholly upon the notion παιδεύω; with the good qualities which the book displays, it is a noteworthy omission that it almost completely passes by τρέφω and the words related to it.

Besides the triad which has already been discussed, the pair of terms ἀνατρέφω and παιδεύω alongside one another is often met with in Greek literature. But from passages such as Plato, *Crito*, 54.A (in which the laws say to Socrates, 'But you wish

---

[1] *Die Apostelgeschichte* (Leipzig, 1939), p. 252.   [2] 5th edn, col. 124.

to live for the sake of your children? You want to bring them up and educate them (αὐτοὺς ἐκθρέψῃς καὶ παιδεύσῃς)? What? will you take them with you to Thessaly, and bring them up and educate them (θρέψεις τε καὶ παιδεύσεις) there? Will you make them strangers to their own country, that you may bestow this benefit on them too? Or supposing that you leave them in Athens, will they be brought up and educated (θρέψονται καὶ παιδεύσονται) better if you are alive, though you are not with them?'),[1] Demosthenes, ad Boeot., 50 (ἀπὸ τοῦ τόκου τῆς προικὸς καὶ τρέφεσθαι καὶ παιδένεσθαι), and Plutarch, Lycurgus, 16.(50.A), (οὐδ' ἐξῆν ἑκάστῳ τρέφειν οὐδὲ παιδεύειν), or de liberis educ., 7.(5.A), (ἐπειδὰν κακῶς μὲν θρέψωσι κακῶς δὲ παιδεύσωσι), not much can be gathered that serves to elucidate the difference between them. From these instances and those already given (pp. 19–27) it can be deduced with a fair degree of certainty that these two notions were not regarded as identical, but that a certain difference was felt between them. But what difference? I have not come upon a definition of these notions in classical antiquity, but I have come upon a very instructive instance of a pointed antithesis, one of the kind that, as R. C. Trench rightly observes,[2] helps towards an accurate definition of notions.

In his great book Against the Christians, which as a whole is lost,[3] Porphyry made a violent outburst concerning Origen. This appears from a passage which Eusebius (Hist. Eccl., VI.xix.7) has preserved. There it is said: 'For Ammonius, being a Christian, and brought up (ἀνατραφείς) by Christian parents, when he gave himself to study and to philosophy (ὅτε τοῦ φρονεῖν καὶ τῆς φιλοσοφίας ἥψατο) straightway conformed to the life required by the laws. But Origen, having been educated (παιδευθείς) as a Greek in Greek literature, went over to the recklessness of the barbarians.'[4] The historical

---

[1] A few other passages in Liddell–Scott, loc. laud., II.1814b; Trans. of F. J. Church in Golden Treasury Series.

[2] New Testament Synonyms (8th edn, London, 1906), p. xvii.

[3] Cf. A. B. Hulen, Porphyry's Work against the Christians, Yale Studies in Religion, Vol. I (New Haven, Conn., 1933).

[4] Trans. of the Nicene and Post-Nicene Library of the Christian Fathers.

correctness of this information is keenly contested by Eusebius (§§9–10), but in the present connection this matter does not need to be further investigated.[1] For our purpose it is sufficient that the two verbs now in question appear here in the same connection and in contrast. Let us set ourselves at the standpoint of the keen and sharp-witted opponent of the Christians, the philosopher who discerned in the Christian Origen a formidable rival, as it were the negation in person of his own position; for indeed, but for Origen, Porphyry would have been able, so he thought, to characterize Christianity as sheer folly below the level of culture, but because of Origen he was precluded from doing so. For Porphyry Greek philosophy was the highest ideal of life, and Christianity a 'barbaric impertinence'.[2] It is within these limits that the lives of Ammonius Saccas, the founder of the Neo-Platonic school to which Porphyry also belonged, and Origen are measured. In Porphyry's judgement the former, in spite of a beginning made in his Christian parental home and foreboding little good, chose the good part when he came into contact with Greek philosophy, whilst Origen, in spite of his study and upbringing in Greek literature, fell among the barbarians.

From this passage the following conclusions may be drawn:

(a) ἀνατραφείς and παιδευθείς may not be put on the same footing or be construed as identical notions. On the contrary the context requires that, although both have to do with human development, the difference in level between the two must be as great as possible.

(b) The παιδεία stands higher than the ἀνατροφή; because of that, the growth of Ammonius, who attained παιδεία in spite of his Christian ἀνατροφή, is the more admirable, and the falling away of Origen, who was already acquainted with Greek παιδεία, the more to be disapproved and the more

---

[1] See on this question the interesting study of M. Hornschuh, 'Das Leben des Origenes', in Zeitschrift für Kirchengeschichte (1960), pp. 13 ff.

[2] The contrast between 'the way of life according to the laws' and a 'barbarous audacity' cannot here be further discussed; see on this J. Jüthner, Hellenen und Barbaren (Wien, 1923).

painful. We need not be surprised that Porphyry used this measuring rod.

(c) The ἀνατρέφειν takes place in the parental home.

(d) The ἀνατρέφειν obviously refers to the *whole* life of the child up to a time of mental maturity (τοῦ φρονεῖν) when he proceeds to acquire a knowledge of philosophy, even if it be but a first beginning of it. [1]

The import, as we have unfolded it here, and the mutual frontiers of these notions are not at all peculiar to Porphyry or to a late stage in the development of the words. They fit completely into the picture of Greek upbringing and education.

In Appendix I a closer investigation is set on foot as to the meaning of (ἀνα)τρέφω. Its results may thus be summarized. The (ἀνα)τρέφειν takes place in the parental home, and in it mother and father play the leading part. 'To feed' in its original meaning, a meaning that always remained closely associated with the verb, is to lay the basis of child-life, but the word also covers all that is bound up with the initial stages of upbringing. The meaning moves very much in the physical sphere, as is understandable at this stage of development; but it does not remain limited to giving suck and supplying food. The beginning rests with the women, whether mother or foster-mother (τροφός), who also through the stories which they tell the child give him an initial mental education. According to Chrysippus this period should continue to the third year. After that, responsibility for the care of the child passes over in a large measure to the father, who, especially in imperial times, if he had the means at his disposal, left it to a slave, the 'pedagogue'. [2] On the father there rests especially the task of teaching the child to read. What the child learns at home relates to

---

[1] ἅπτομαι = to attach oneself to, to undertake, to be engaged on; cf. Liddell–Scott, I.231, and Plutarch, *De liberis educandis*, 20.(14.B): 'Here we may take the example of Eurydice, who, although she was an Illyrian and so thrice a barbarian, yet applied herself (ἥψατο) to learning when she was well advanced in years, that she might teach her children.'

[2] See Boulogne, *De plaats van de paedagogus in de Romeinse cultuur*, p. 31.

the tongue, the customs, the formation of character, and the elementary duties towards elders, the gods, and the State. Here example works powerfully, and therefore it matters supremely how parents conduct themselves and to whom they entrust their children. This continues until the child goes to school and is put into the hands of teachers who look after the παιδεύειν, the typical intellectual moulding of the spirit in virtue through instruction and in general culture by means of study.

The Greek use of words for the guidance of child-life to the adult stage is in this respect constant from the time of Plato onwards. From this we may draw the following conclusions:

(a) When mention is made of (ἀνα)τρέφω, it is always the sphere of the parental home that is in view.

(b) There is no reason to assume two nuances for ἀνατρέφω, as Bauer did by distinguishing between physical and mental upbringing; the notion embraces both these aspects.

(c) Lake–Cadbury's and Grosheide's description of the difference between ἀνατρέφω and παιδεύω as being the difference between physical and mental training is insufficient, because that would make it possible for the two to take place at the same time, whereas from the texts it is apparent that these words indicate stages on life's way *that follow one another*, first a stage in the home and after that another stage under the guidance of teachers; the first is translated by 'upbringing', the second by 'education'.

The triad of terms, about which we have already spoken (pp. 19 ff) as an established series, has thus clear reference to three successive stages of human development up to the adult stage and registers the salient points which are decisive for it. Sometimes in a simple summing up and sometimes again as the thread for a more detailed discussion, as in Philo, Plutarch, and Quintilian, [1] there are noted: the γένεσις (not merely the fact of the birth, but also the circumstances in which it took place and the tendency which it gave), the (ἀνα)τροφή (with its

---

[1] It is possible that, under the influence of rhetoric, the originally short statement was used later as a '*leit-motiv*' for elaborate descriptions.

sphere in the home and the possibilities of growth) and the παιδεύσις (the intellectual culture).

(4) That this schema was also known to Luke is evident from Acts 7²⁰⁻², as has already been observed on page 28. It is desirable to look at this passage in still more detail. In the discourse of Stephen, the Hellenist (7²⁰ ᶠᶠ), it is said: 'In which time Moses was born (ἐγγενήθη), and was exceeding fair, and was brought up (ἀνετράφη) in his father's house three months; and when he was cast out (ἐκτεθέντος δὲ αὐτοῦ), Pharaoh's daughter took him up, and brought him up (ἀνεθρέψατο) as her own son. And Moses was learned (ἐπαιδεύθη) in all the wisdom of the Egyptians.' Here, then, mention is made first of all of Moses' birth. Next we are told that he was brought up by his parents, and then, what may well appear impossible (cf. verse 19), that the daughter of Pharaoh took over the role of the parents. Luke uses here the typical term for 'to expose a foundling',[1] and in illustration of his statements that Pharaoh's daughter adopted him and brought him up as her own son there may be cited these words of Boulogne: 'One who took a foundling to himself fulfilled the whole task of a parent' — words written with reference to a passage in Suetonius but without any thought of Acts.[2] In view of the Greek usage, there is, then, not the least reason to import here two shades of meaning into the notion, as Bauer wished to do. Finally, there comes in verse 22 the third phase, the instruction in the wisdom of the Egyptians indicated by the typical παιδεία.

If we compare this description of Moses' youth with the version of it in the Old Testament (Ex 2¹⁻¹⁰), the difference strikes us at once. There, for example, 'instruction' is not mentioned at all, and here the use of παιδεύω (cf. p. 28 above) and

---

[1] J. H. Moulton–G. Milligan, The Vocabulary of the Greek Testament (London, 1930), p. 199, s.v., and Liddell–Scott, Vol. I, s.v.

[2] Boulogne, De plaats van de paedagogus in de Romeinse cultuur, p. 57. Bauer, Griechisch-deutsches Wörterbuch zu den Schriften des Neuen Testaments (5th edn), col. 124, cites Eutecnius, 4, p. 41.18: 'he took Dionysus out of the small chest and brought him up'; cf. also Heliodorus, Aethiopica, X.iv.1: 'for he adopted the exposed child and brought her up secretly'.

ἐκτίθημι (see above) points to Hellenistic terminology. From this it may well be concluded that Luke has reproduced the story in a way that was current in his day and has made use of a schema that was familiar to Greek readers. Joachim Jeremias has pointed out that the idea of 'instruction in Egypt' is to be found only in Hellenistic legends about Moses.[1] To me, however, it seems probable, not that we have here to do with a definitely fixed legend, but that in giving the history both Luke and Philo made use for the sake of their Hellenistic readers of the self-same sort of schema and style.

It will be interesting, with a view to the speech-usage, also to cite here for the purposes of comparison the versions of the youth of Moses given in Philo and Josephus.

PHILO, *de Vita Mosis*, liber I (divisions according to the edition of Cohn–Wendland, IV.120 ff.): 'Moses', it is stated, 'was by race a Chaldaean, but he was born (ἐγγενήθη) and brought up (ἐτράφη) in Egypt' (§5). We are then told why his forefathers had come to Egypt, and concerning his parents that 'his father and mother were among the most excellent persons of their time' (§7). A new element is brought into the account with the words: 'he was thought worthy of being brought up (τροφῆς) in the royal palace' (§8). Because of his beauty, his parents after his birth (γεννηθείς), scorned the command of the tyrant, and he was secretly suckled at home (γαλακτοτροφηθῆναι, §9); when this appeared to be no longer possible, his parents exposed him with tears as a foundling (ἐκτιθέασι, §10), and concerning the period during which they had kept him at home they say: ἀνεθρέψαμεν (§11). After that we are told in detail how the childless daughter of Pharaoh found him, recognized him as one of the Hebrew children and 'took counsel with herself regarding his upbringing (τροφῆς), because she found it dangerous to bring him to the king at once' (§15). His mother then became his foster-mother (γαλακτοτροφηθῆναι: τροφεύσειν), thanks to the 'providence of God who thus made the

---

[1] Μωυσῆς in G. Kittel, *Theologisches Wörterbuch zum Neuen Testament* (Stuttgart o. J., 1942), IV.870 (an excellent article).

earliest upbringing (τροφάς) of the child to accord with the genuine course of nature' (§§16–17). When he was weaned, his μήτηρ ἅμα καὶ τροφός brought him to the princess, who feigned pregnancy and adopted him as her son (§§18–19). How he then fared in the palace is outlined in the following words: 'Therefore being now thought worthy of a royal upbringing (τροφῆς) and attendance, he was not, like a mere child, long delighted with games and objects of amusement and laughter, even though those who had undertaken the care of him allowed him times for relaxation and never behaved in any stern way to him; but his deportment was modest and dignified, and he attended diligently to everything he heard and saw that could tend to the improvement of his mind' (§20). In §21 we are then told that he obtained Egyptian and Greek teachers (note the transition: διδάσκαλοι δ᾽ εὐθὺς ἀλλαχόθεν ἄλλοι παρῆσαν). His course of study, set out in §23, was typically Greek in composition (τὴν δ᾽ ἄλλην ἐγκύκλιον παιδείαν), yet such that really everything that was to be known became his intellectual possession. His upbringing was now complete; 'and when he had passed the bounds of the age of boyhood' (§25), he did not give himself over to the dissolute lusts to which his high position made it possible for him to yield himself, but was σώφρων (§§25–9). He was not puffed up with good fortune and did not look down upon his own people and their customs, as often happens:[1] for men 'disdain their relatives and friends, and transgress the laws according to which they were born (ἐγενήθησαν) and brought up (ἐτράφησαν); and having departed from their accustomed mode of life, they overturn their national hereditary customs to which no just blame whatever is attached' (§31). But Moses 'admired the education (παιδείαν) of his kinsmen and ancestors' (§32).

[1] Behaviour which involved 'the despising of the ancestral customs' was also for a Greek extremely contemptible: to learn these was in fact part of the rudiments of the domestic upbringing (cf. p. 65 below). For a Jew such behaviour signified the forsaking of the law of God. L. Cohn (*Die Werke Philos von Alexandria* [Breslau, 1931], p. 229, note 2) sees here, probably quite correctly, a repercussion of happenings which had taken place in Philo's own family.

That ends Philo's version of Exodus 2¹⁻¹⁰. It is striking that here the triple schema is actually used twice: first in §§5–24 (namely, 5–7, birth; 8–20, ἀνατροφή in a double sense; 20–4, παιδεία), and secondly in §§31–2. It has been pointed out that in the case of Moses more is said of ἀνάμνησις than of μάθησις: here he is portrayed rather as a critical investigator of every-thing than as a pupil (§24). But in the violent outburst against the 'lucky persons' who transgress the first principles of ἀνατροφή Moses is praised. In his case 'birth, upbringing, and education' were all on the same footing, namely, that of the ancestral religion; he adhered to the Jewish παιδεία and not to that of the Egyptians.[1] This seeming contrariety in Philo's description has undoubtedly not only the potency of 'an application of the sermon' but also that of a polemical spear-head; Moses was indeed initiated into all knowledge — but his παιδεία was essentially Jewish. Here a typical difference can be seen between this account and the one in Acts 7. In all circumstances Philo is an apologist for Judaism; in Acts 7²⁰ ᶠᶠ this note is lacking.

JOSEPHUS (*Antiq. Jud.*, II.ix.3–x.1.§§210–38) gives quite a different paraphrase. According to him, the father of Moses was in great distress before the child's birth as to what he should do, but in a dream God reassured him, saying that the child whose birth the Egyptians feared would be his own child, but that he would escape from those who lay in wait for him, and having grown up (τραφεὶς δὲ παραδόξως) would deliver the Hebrews and obtain for himself an everlasting name. The circumstances under which Moses' *birth* took place are de-scribed in §§210–18. After that there follows an account of how he was brought up for three months in the parental home

---

[1] See also what is said in the end of §32: 'Considering the things that were thought good among those who had adopted him as spurious, even though in consequence of the present state of affairs they might have a brilliant appearance, and considering the things that were thought good by his natural parents as at all events akin to himself and genuinely good, even though they might for a short time be somewhat obscure.'

(§218: καὶ τρεῖς μὲν μῆνας παρ' αὐτοῖς τρέφουσι λανθάνοντες),
and of how from sheer necessity but with trust in God's care
his parents exposed him as a foundling. After that he was
found by Thermouthis the daughter of Pharaoh (§§219–24),
for 'God had taken such great care in the formation of Moses,
that He caused him to be thought worthy of being brought up
and provided for by those who had made the most dreadful
resolves, on account of their fear of his birth, to destroy the
rest of the Hebrew nation' (§225). Moses refused the breast-
feeding of Egyptian women, whereupon, without its being
known, Moses' own mother appeared as his foster-mother
(§227): 'At the queen's desire the nursing (τροφήν) of the child
was entirely entrusted to the mother.' In §230 there follows an
account of how Moses was in understanding far in advance of
his age and of what he showed in his games that contained a
promise for the future. Of his third year, it is said in particular
(cf. the advice of Chrysippus referred to on p. 64 below) that
in it 'God also made him wonderfully tall' (§231). As she was
herself childless, Thermouthis adopted Moses as her son (§232
παῖδα ποιεῖται), in which connection along with other things
she said: 'I have brought up (ἀναθρεψαμένη) a child who
is of divine form and of a generous mind.' When she put
Moses on Pharaoh's knees, he seized his crown, threw it
on the ground and trampled upon it, an act in which the
Egyptians saw a token of evil; but Thermouthis knew how to
avert disaster. In §236 it is then said: 'He was therefore
brought up (ἐτρέφετο) with great care;' the Jews were full of
good hope, 'but the Egyptians were suspicious of what would
follow this his upbringing (ἀνατροφήν)' (§237). Josephus com-
pletes the account of the youth of Moses with the information:
'Moses therefore (μὲν οὖν), when he was born, was brought up
(τραφείς) in the foregoing manner, and came to the age of
maturity' (§238).

It is surprising that in this account the 'instruction' of the
Egyptians is not mentioned with a single word. Where we
should expect it, Josephus speaks of ἀνατροφή. At the end of his

argument he tenders a noteworthy variant of the threefold formula. [1] This is of course not accidental, being connected not with the fact that the account in Exodus 2 does not mention this instruction, but with the apologetic purpose which Josephus pursues in his *Antiquities*. The true παιδεία is for him instruction in the Torah (the Law); see below. Finally, it may be pointed out that again (ἀνα)τροφή is clearly used not merely of bodily nutrition but of the whole stay in the foster-family (p. 35 above).

In this connection there may be cited a few lines of the Jewish tragic poet Ezekiel (second century B.C.) [2] which are preserved in Eusebius, *Praep. Evang.*, IX.28, and in which 'upbringing' and 'instruction' are mentioned side by side:

> So when my time of infancy was past,
> My mother led me to the princess' home,
> But first she told me all the tale, my birth
> And kindred, and God's gifts of old.
> The princess then through all my boyhood's years,
> As I had been a son of her own womb
> In royal state and learning nurtured me
> (τροφαῖσι βασιλικαῖσι καὶ παιδεύμασιν
> ἅπανθ᾽ ὑπισχνεῖθ᾽,). [3]

From Acts 7^{20-2} it is, then, clearly apparent that for the writer of Acts also the ἀνατροφή took place in the sphere of the home and was certainly different from the παιδεύειν which was given by others.

---

[1] Here he uses the word οὖν, cf. with regard to this my observations in '1 Clement 34 and the "Sanctus"' in *Vigiliae Christianae*, V.(1951).221–2; this clearly registers a sort of conclusion from the foregoing, and a transition, on the basis of this conclusion, to what is new.

[2] On the date of Ezekiel Tragicus, see R. H. Pfeiffer, *History of New Testament Times* (New York, 1949), p. 211.

[3] Trans. of E. H. Gifford. Cf. J. Wiencke, *Ezechielis Judaei poetae Alexandrini fabulae quae inscribitur ΕΧΑΓΩΓΗ*, Monasterii Westphalorum, 1931, p. 51 f.: 'quibus de rebus (verses 34–5) nihil est in Sacra Scriptura, poeta autem haec narrat, ut Mosis mores — id quod prologi est — atque naturam accuratius pingat … τροφαί sunt corporis victus cultusque. παιδεύμα … id quod educatur … deinde institutio vel disciplina'.

(5) Before we apply to the interpretation of Acts 22³ what we have found about the meaning of the terms used by Luke, a few words ought to be said about the Jewish upbringing.[1]

According to Josephus (c. Apionem, I.12.§60) the Jews applied themselves above all things to παιδοτροφία. Here there is mentioned first the task of the mother or wet-nurse; the giving suck continued for a long time, namely for two to three years.[2] After that the father imparted to the child the first rudiments of reading; instruction in the Law began as soon as possible, and in that instruction the teaching of Jewish customs had a special place.[3] It was also the duty of the father to teach his son a trade. Probably there were already schools in the time of the New Testament, but education in them was not compulsory.[4] In this connection it is striking that Luke relates of Jesus: ἦλθεν εἰς Ναζαρά, οὗ ἦν (ἀνα)τεθραμμένος (4¹⁶);[5] nothing is said here about instruction in school, whereas in Acts Luke uses the 'triad'; as comparison with the other Synoptists shows, this note is an observation of his own. Joshua ben Gamaliel is supposed to have established compulsory education, beginning with the sixth or seventh year.[6]

---

[1] See on this E. Schürer, Geschichte des jüdischen Volkes im Zeitalter Jesu Christi (4th edn, Leipzig, 1907), II.492–7; S. Krauss, Talmudische Archäologie (Leipzig, 1911–12), II.1–23, III.199–239; G. F. Moore, Judaism (Cambridge, Mass., 1927), I.309 ff; W. Jentsch, Urchristliches Erziehungsdenken, pp. 117–39.

[2] Krauss, Talmudische Archäologie, II.9. See 2 Maccabees 7²⁷: 'My son, have pity upon me that carried thee nine months in my womb, and gave thee suck three years'; also the note of F. M. Abel, Les livres des Maccabées (Paris, 1949), in loc., pp. 379–80; and cf. below, p. 64.

[3] Krauss, ibid. III.229: 'Among the Jews in all ages a principal means of education has been the training in customs and the guidance (חנוך) received in the parental home.'

[4] Schürer, Geschichte des jüdischen Volkes im Zeitalter Jesu Christi, II.494.

[5] The manuscripts have both readings; see the apparatus in Nestle, Novum Testamentum Graece, in loc.

[6] The statement of the Babylonian Talmud (Baba Bathra, fol. 21a) is well known: 'Rab Judah said in the name of the Rabbi: Truly it may be remembered to this man's credit! Joshua ben Gamla is his name. If he had not lived, the law would have been forgotten in Israel. For at first, he who had a father was taught the law by him, he who had none did not learn the law. . . . Afterwards it was ordained that teachers of

Whoever wished could of course proceed after that to specialize further in the knowledge of the Law under a rabbi. The sequence of study is known from the Mishna, *Pirke Aboth*, V.21, a passage on the basis of which the statement is often made that Paul went to Jerusalem in his fifteenth year: 'In the fifth year to the Bible, in the tenth to the Mishna, in the thirteenth to the commandments, in the fifteenth to the Talmud, in the eighteenth to marriage.'[1]

In the nature of things, this course of upbringing, as can be clearly seen, was parallel to the Greek. First there was the parental upbringing, by which the child was trained in the ancestral customs and learned the rudiments of reading and writing. After that there was (possibly) a broadening of knowledge under professional teachers.[2] But so far as I know, no form of the triad as it appears in Greek literature occurs in the Old Testament or in the rabbinical writings.

It is indeed possible to recover this series, applied to the Jewish upbringing, in Philo, *Legatio ad Gaium*, 16.§115: 'For he regarded the Jews with most special suspicion, as if they were the only persons who cherished wishes opposed to his and who had been taught, so to speak, from the cradle[3] by their parents, teachers, and those who brought them up, even before being instructed in the sacred laws and the unwritten customs, to believe in God the one Father and Creator of the world', and in Josephus, *c. Apionem*, II.25.§204: 'Nay indeed,

boys should be appointed in Jerusalem. . . . But he who had a father was sent to school by him, he who had none did not go there. Then it was ordained that teachers should be appointed in every province, and that boys of the age of sixteen or seventeen should be sent to them. But he whose teacher was angry with him ran away, till Joshua ben Gamla came and enacted that teachers should be appointed in every province and in every town, and children of six or seven years old brought to them.' According to Schürer (*Geschichte des jüdischen Volkes im Zeitalter Jesu Christi*, p. 494) this Joshua lived as high priest *c.* A.D. 65. We see that the principal concern was the study of the Law.

[1] Ed. K. Marti–G. Beer (Giessen, 1927), pp. 152–3.

[2] Schürer, *Geschichte des jüdischen Volkes im Zeitalter Jesu Christi*, pp. 384–6.

[3] Note that ἐξ αὐτῶν σπαργάνων = from the cradle. Cf. p. 67 below, where the same expression occurs in this connection. Cf. also 2 Timothy 3[15].

he (namely Moses) did not permit us to make festivals at the births of our children, and thereby afford occasions of drinking to excess; but he ordained that the very beginning of our up-bringing should be immediately directed to sobriety. He also commanded us to teach (παιδεύειν) our children letters, and to make them acquainted with the laws and with the deeds of their forefathers — with the latter that they might imitate them, and with the former that growing up with them they might not transgress them nor have the excuse of ignorance.'[1]

In the latter passage, however, it is not clear with whom the παιδεύειν rests, whether with parents or with teachers. This points to a difference between Jewish and Greek upbringing. What Plato and Plutarch say about the difference, indeed the contrast, between education at home and education under teachers[2] cannot be said of Jewish instruction. Among the Jews the παιδεία did not move on a level different from that of the (ἀνα)τροφή. The whole of life from its very beginning, even at home, was defined by the Law and its application, and to that the instruction given by teachers imparted depth and breadth.[3] This secured continuity where the Greek 'paideia' sometimes occasioned a break. Nevertheless it was of course also possible, especially when what was in mind was the con-tinued study of the Law, to apply to the Jewish situation the two distinguishing notions of (ἀνα)τρέφειν and παιδεύειν.

[1] The text followed here is that of Th. Reinach, Flavius Josèphe, Contre Apion (Paris, 1930); cf. also Schürer, Geschichte des jüdischen Volkes im Zeitalter Jesu Christi, II.492, note 18. Cf. with this the version which Josephus gives of the instruction in a letter of Artaxerxes to Ezra, 1 Esdras 8²³⁻⁴ (LXX): 'Ordain judges and justices, that they may judge in all Syria and Phoenicia all those that know the law of thy God; and those that know it not thou shalt teach. And whosoever shall transgress the law of thy God and of the king shall be punished diligently' = Josephus, Ant. Jud., XI.§§129–30: 'Teach those who are ignorant of it (the Law) that if any one of thy countrymen transgress the law of God or that of the king, he may be punished as not trans-gressing it out of ignorance, but as one that knows it indeed, but boldly despises and contemns it. And such shall be punished.'

[2] See p. 27 and p. 64.

[3] For the instruction to parents to teach their children the com-mandments of the Law, see Deuteronomy 4⁹⁻¹⁰. By doing so one

D

(6) If now we read Acts 22³ in the light of the foregoing discussion of the linguistic usage, the following are the conclusions to which we must come:

(a) Luke here describes the course and development of Paul's life in a terminology which was familiar to his Hellenistic readers and which suited the Jewish situation.

(b) In this context ἀνατεθραμμένος can refer only to Paul's upbringing in the home of his parents from the earliest years of his childhood until he was of school age; πεπαιδευμένος refers to the instruction which he received in accordance with Eastern custom[1] 'at the feet of' Gamaliel.

(c) This of itself solves the problem about the punctuation (see pp. 17–18 above). Greek readers, who knew the significance of ἀνατρέφω in such a context, would of course have regarded it as quite foolish to connect 'at the feet of Gamaliel' with that word. This is not undone by any considerations about the rhythm of the sentence. The name Gamaliel in its third member has probably been brought forward in order that full emphasis may fall upon it at once. Steinmann has rightly observed that although the matter of the punctuation appears to be a trifle, it is in fact very important for the interpretation; but in saying this he has passed judgement on himself, for he has not adequately investigated the range of the Greek verbs.

(d) From the contrast between Tarsus as the place of birth and Jerusalem as the city of the ἀνατροφή (upbringing in the home-circle) and the παιδεία (study under Gamaliel), it is clear that *according to this text Paul spent the years of his youth completely in Jerusalem*; not a single word is breathed about an upbringing in Tarsus. 'I am a Jew, born at Tarsus in Cilicia, but my parental home, where I received my early upbringing, was in this city (Jerusalem); and under Gamaliel, a person well-known to you, I received a strict

acquired 'wisdom'; cf. G. F. Moore, *Judaism*, pp. 312 ff, and W. Gutbrod, in Kittel, *Theologisches Wörterbuch zum Neuen Testament*, IV.1049–50.
¹ See on this the Commentary of Strack–Billerbeck, II.763–5.

training as a Pharisee,[1] so that I was a zealot for God's cause as ye all are today' — that is how, paraphrasing them somewhat, we ought to render the words of this verse.[2]

[1] As my colleague J. H. Waszink, Leyden, has observed, the second portion of the sentence is chiastic in construction.

[2] The exegesis as proposed in the foregoing discussion is followed in the voluminous and important commentary of E. Haenchen (*Die Apostelgeschichte* [12th edn, Göttingen, 1959], p. 554, note I), who summarizes the arguments, though he is rather sceptical with regard to the historical trustworthiness of Luke. It is also found, but without the argument of the literary schema, in J. Dupont (*Les Actes des Apôtres* [Paris, 1954], p. 183), who adds in note *c*: 'Paul lets us understand that he came to Jerusalem when still an infant.' The right translation, but without comments, is also in F. F. Bruce, *The Book of the Acts* (Edinburgh, 1954), p. 440, and C. S. C. Williams, *The Acts of the Apostles* (London, 1957), p. 243.

Other Texts Connected with Paul's Youth

BESIDES Acts 22³, which, as has already been observed on p. 14, is the only text giving *concrete* data for Paul's youth, we have to examine a few other passages which are connected or are brought into connection with it.

(1) In Acts 26⁴⁻⁵, in his defence before Agrippa, Paul brings forward for discussion the course of his life. The first point that he makes in his apologia is that the Jews, if they be willing, can testify concerning him that he has lived as a Pharisee,[1] for they know him. This is expressed as follows:

τὴν μὲν οὖν βίωσίν μου ἐκ νεότητος τὴν ἀπ' ἀρχῆς γενομένην ἐν τῷ ἔθνει μου ἔν τε Ἱεροσολύμοις ἴσασι πάντες Ἰουδαῖοι, προγινώσκοντές με ἄνωθεν, ἐὰν θέλωσι μαρτυρεῖν, ὅτι κατὰ τὴν ἀκριβεστάτην αἵρεσιν τῆς ἡμετέρας θρησκείας ἔζησα Φαρισαῖος.

The wording is somewhat exuberant,[2] but through its being so one point is heavily underlined, namely that the Jews have known him already for a long time. The Jews meant here are of course those present from Jerusalem (cf. 26² with 25⁷ and ¹⁴): the accusers must themselves appear as witnesses for the defence. (If Paul had spent the earliest years of his life in Tarsus, an appeal to Jews who had known him there would at this moment have been meaningless.) Paul says that these accusers have known him from his youth. The term

---

[1] Cf. Acts 22³, ⁶, Galatians 1¹³, Philippians 3⁵. A. Schlatter, *Die Theologie des Judentums nach dem Bericht des Josephus* (Gütersloh, 1932), p. 205: 'The term ἀκρίβεια frequently denotes the aim of Pharisaism.'

[2] Preuschen (*Die Apostelgeschichte*, p. 145) calls it intolerable without giving his reasons for doing so.

νεότης can be used for 'youth in general',[1] and here that meaning of it is indicated more precisely by ἀπ' ἀρχῆς and also by προγινώσκοντες ἄνωθεν. This ἄνωθεν does not mean simply 'for a long time'[2] but is parallel to ἀπ' ἀρχῆς, and like the former phrase means 'from the beginning'.[3] In other words, the Jerusalem Jews could survey Paul's life onwards from the earliest days of his youth. That agrees excellently with the exegesis given above of Acts 22³ and confirms it in an unexpected way. In this situation it would surely have been complete madness on Paul's part to have made this defence if it had referred only to his life after his tenth or fifteenth year,[4] for then his argument could have been invalidated with the comment: 'When you came to Jerusalem, you were already spoilt.'

Everything then would be in complete agreement if there was not a tiny word, namely τε, in the expression ἔν τε Ἱεροσολύμοις, which seems to point in another direction. This can certainly be interpreted, as indeed it most often is interpreted, by the phrase 'among my people and in Jerusalem', the first half of which points to Cilicia.[5] But although this fits in with the general opinion about the place of Paul's youth, it conflicts with the clear sense of the words of Acts 22³. Textually, however, this τε has no firm standing,[6] although

---

[1] Grosheide, *De Handelingen der Apostelen*, p. 363: 'Not childhood years, but young years, 1 Timothy 4¹²'; cf. Bauer, *Griechisch-deutsches Wörterbuch zu den Schriften des Neuen Testaments* (5th edn), col. 1061.

[2] So Lake–Cadbury (*Beginnings of Christianity*, IV.315), although they also recognize that the two words can be synonymous. The reason for their judgement is not quite clear to me, and is apparently determined by their understanding of Acts 22³. Attention should also be paid to the prefix προ.

[3] See Luke 1³; Liddell–Scott, *A Greek-English Lexicon*, I.169, s.v. II, and Bauer (5th edn), col. 153, sub. 2 (there does not seem to me to be the least reason for such a distinction as Bauer draws in *a* and *b*). An interesting parallel is afforded by Eusebius (*Praeparatio Evangelica*, VII.3.2): 'For of all mankind these (the Hebrews) were the first and sole people who from the beginning (ἄνωθεν), from the first foundation of social life, . . .'

[4] As must be assumed on the usual understanding of Acts 22³, see p. 7 above.

[5] So Zahn and Lake–Cadbury in their commentaries, in loc.

[6] See J. H. Ropes in his edition of Acts, *The Beginnings of Christianity*, III.(1926).234.

the oldest witnesses certainly point in a direction favourable to its retention. It is a conjunction for which Luke — as an exception, it may be said, among the New Testament writers — has a preference.[1] Moreover, as Zahn observes,[2] since it creates an exegetical puzzle, it is more likely that it has been deleted by later scribes than that it has been added. The statement of Steinmann[3] that if 'among my people' and 'in Jerusalem' were connected, the words would lack cogency, is not convincing. No more satisfying is the observation of Zahn[4] that it is essentially foolish to add 'in Jerusalem' to ἔθνος understood as 'people', for which reason he gives to ἔθνος the meaning 'eparchy'; for elsewhere in Acts this word in the mouth of Paul is used for 'the Jewish people' (24^{17}, 28^{19}),[5] and we cannot see why it should have another meaning here. With regard to the use of τε, it may be observed that many a time it is used in Greek without any special reason,[6] and that it 'is used in descriptions of particular places or things, when attention is called to their peculiar or characteristic features'.[7] In the New Testament reference may be made, for example, to Acts 6^7, 11^{21}, 15^{39}, where its use is explicative ('yes indeed', and 'certainly'; cf. also Hebrews 9^1). That fits in here exactly. It was possible to check the course of Paul's life from its very

[1] See the concordance, s.v. τε, and F. Blass–A. Debrunner, *Grammatik des neutestamentlichen Griechisch* (7th edn, Göttingen, 1943), p. 201.

[2] Zahn, *Die Apostelgeschichte*, p. 797.

[3] Steinmann, *Zum Werdegang des Paulus, die Jugendzeit in Tarsus*, p. 28. It may be observed here that through beginning his discussion of Paul's youth with an exegesis of Acts 26^{4-5} and not of 22^3 — one of several blunders in his interpretation — Steinmann has landed on a wrong track.

[4] Zahn, *Die Apostelgeschichte*, p. 797.

[5] Cf. K. L. Schmidt in Kittel, *Theologisches Wörterbuch zum Neuen Testament*, II.366; Josephus also uses the word ἔθνος regularly for the 'Jewish people'.

[6] L. Radermacher, *Neutestamentliche Grammatik* (2nd edn, Tübingen, 1925), p. 5.

[7] Liddell–Scott, *A Greek-English Lexicon*, II.1764.B.8. An interesting example of the use of τε in Josephus, *Contra Apionem*, I.15.§98: 'not to be injurious to the Queen, the mother of his children (τὴν βασιλίδα μητέρα τε τῶν τέκνων)'; see §100, which proves that the same person is meant.

first beginning, not merely among his own people who lived scattered everywhere, but actually[1] in Jerusalem itself. In consequence the Jews from Jerusalem could not fail to do so. On closer examination, then, there appears to be no reason at all to assume a contradiction between 22³ and 26⁴⁻⁵. When we consider this part of Paul's reasoning before Agrippa, we find that its content agrees wonderfully well with the information given in Chapter 22.

(2) In Acts 9¹¹ Paul is referred to as 'a man of Tarsus', and to this in 21³⁹ he himself, in introducing himself to the chiliarch, adds 'a citizen of a city of Cilicia that is not without renown'. These passages are often brought forward in discussions of Paul's youth, but they say nothing more than what is said in 22³, namely that he was born in Tarsus. It is not said that in the days of his youth he had lived there for more than ten years. It may indeed well be assumed that especially in Jerusalem he was also known as 'Saul of Tarsus', since of course there were other men there who bore the name Saul. With this we may compare Simon the Cyrenian (Mk 15²¹ = Mt 27³² = Lk 23²⁶), the name of a man who came from the fields and so was a dweller in Jerusalem, but who continued still to bear the name of the land of his origin. This parallel stands out in still stronger relief in the light of Acts 6⁹: ἀνέστησαν δέ τινες τῶν ἐκ τῆς συναγωγῆς τῆς λεγομένης Λιβερτίνων καὶ Κυρηναίων καὶ Ἀλεξανδρέων καὶ τῶν ἀπὸ Κιλικίας καὶ Ἀσίας συζητοῦντες τῷ Στεφάνῳ. Exactly how this text ought to be divided (have we to do here with one, two, or five synagogues?) does not concern us here.[2] What is important for our investigation is that it appears that all sorts of men of non-Palestinian birth or descent, among whom with others Cyrenians and Cilicians are named, had synagogues of their own in Jerusalem. Later on, as one standing by Stephen's opponents, Paul also is named (7⁵⁸).

---

[1] So also Beyer and Bauernfeind, who (in their commentaries, in loc.) translate 'and indeed'.

[2] See the commentaries on this question and Strack–Billerbeck, *Kommentar zum Neuen Testament aus Talmud und Midrasch*, II.661–5.

The fact that Paul, when confronted with the occupying Roman power, appealed to his right as a citizen of Tarsus (21^{39}), to his right as a Roman citizen by birth [1] (22^{25-8}; cf. also 16^{37-40}), and to his derivation from the province of Cilicia (23^{34}, before Felix) is not to the purpose so far as our problem is concerned. Being regarded at the time as a rebel (cf. 21^{38}), he proceeded to make what in my opinion was an entirely lawful use of the citizen-right which he possessed. His doing so does not affect the question whether he was in Tarsus for a long or a short time. Whether or not he spent his youth in Jerusalem is altogether irrelevant; though to confess that he had done so would have done him harm in the eyes of the Romans rather than good. [2]

(3) The information given in Acts 18^3 that by trade Paul was a σκηνοποιός has been connected with his Tarsus origin, because Cilician wool was worked up in Tarsus. If we ignore all dispute about what this trade was (tentmaker, or leather-worker as Grosheide and Zahn [3] explain it), this verse, taken by itself, would provide perhaps a little evidence to suggest that Paul spent the years of his youth in Tarsus. But he could just as fittingly have learned this trade elsewhere; or he might have been taught it by his father who was perhaps himself a tent-maker who had learned his trade in Tarsus. This passage has no evidential value for the problem handled here.

---

[1] See on this A. Souter, 'Citizenship', in Hastings, *Dictionary of the Apostolic Church* (Edinburgh, 1915), I.212–13.

[2] This paragraph, which was already in the first edition, offers, I think, a sufficient explanation of the difficulties expressed by B. Rigaux in his extensive and stimulating commentary, *Saint Paul, Les Epîtres aux Thessaloniciens* (Paris–Gembloux, 1956), p. 5. It is true that, as Rigaux remarks, Paul's return to Tarsus (Acts 9^{30}; cf. 11^{25}) shows that his origin there 'was more than a nominal connection with that city of Cilicia'. But I fail to see that this fact tells against my exegesis of Acts 22^3. Paul's connection with Tarsus may have been very strong, and he was a citizen there; but that does not exclude the possibility that he lived from his earliest boyhood in Jerusalem, and that is what Acts 22^3 says.

[3] See their commentaries, in loc.

(4) Acts 23[16] is used by Zahn (see p. 29 above) to outline further the picture of Paul's youth. Apart from what has already been said about this, it should be regarded as settled that we do not know how Paul's sister came to Jerusalem or that she herself lived there.[1] The verse says nothing against the view that Paul's youth was spent in the parental home in Jerusalem. If it be assumed that the sister did indeed live in Jerusalem as a married woman, it is precisely our view that Paul's family moved there in his youth which makes such an assumption reasonable and likely.

(5) In the autobiographical portion of Galatians 1, only verse 15 refers to Paul's youth, and it throws no light on the present question; no more does Philippians 3[5]. These verses do not conflict with the proposed explanation of Acts 22[3] any more than they speak in its favour.

[1] So correctly, A. Steinmann, *Die Apostelgeschichte* (4th edn, Bonn, 1934), p. 270: It cannot be made out whether the sister lived in Jerusalem or was there on a pilgrimage, or whether the son studied in Jerusalem or was there for other reasons.

Conclusion and Perspectives

THE STARTING-POINT of our investigation was the question of where Paul spent the years of his youth. On the basis of the clear witness of Acts 22³, confirmed by 26⁴⁻⁵ (other data are not at our service), only one answer is possible: *in opposition to the prevailing opinion about this, it must be concluded that although Paul was born in Tarsus, it was in Jerusalem that he received his upbringing in the parental home just as it was in Jerusalem that he received his later schooling for the rabbinate.* When and why his parents removed to Jerusalem remains concealed from us because of lack of data. But the use of the word ἀνατεθραμμένος necessitates the supposition that this removal took place quite early in Paul's life, apparently before he could peep round the corner of the door and certainly before he went roaming on the street.

Here the comment may perhaps be made that this information, as appears from the wording, comes from the pen of Luke. Is his report to be trusted? What here ought to be in the forefront is the fact that no other texts are at our disposal. According to Joh. Weiss and Knopf the fact-content of this passage is 'unassailable'.[1] An objection, such as that of Bultmann,[2] to Paul's training in Jerusalem, on the ground that this would conflict with Galatians 1²², is hardly tenable, for Paul speaks there about a later time, and it can hardly be assumed that in a city like Jerusalem everyone would know definitely all the pupils of the rabbis (besides in Galatians 1²² it is 'the churches of Judaea' that are mentioned); in this objection no account at all is taken of the realities of everyday life. The

[1] Joh. Weiss, *Das Urchristentum* (Göttingen, 1917), p. 131; R. Knopf, 'Apostelgeschichte', in *Die Schriften des Neuen Testaments* (3rd edn), p. 125.
[2] In *Religion in Geschichte und Gegenwart* (2nd edn), Vol. IV, cols. 1020-1.

witness of Acts 22³, 23⁶ and 26⁵ agrees here with that of Philippians 3⁵.[1] Indeed it can be said in general that the present assessment of the trustworthiness of Luke as a writer of history is high.[2] It cannot be deduced from the mere fact that, like ancient historiographers generally, he puts into the mouth of his characters speeches which they are thought to have delivered on certain occasions,[3] that in matters of fact the content of these speeches has been invented. Some time ago H. Bolkestein pointed out that Livy's account of the Bacchanalia in Rome 'is altogether correct and trustworthy so far as matters of fact are concerned, and that he has also reproduced with excellent judgement the purport of the measures that were taken', as is apparent from an inscription that has been recovered.[4] Moreover, we cannot see for what reasons Luke would have invented this report and why he would so readily have constructed a close connection between Paul at the outset of his life and Judaism.[5] Assuming that the writer

[1] The wording is, however, so different and so much more detailed in Acts that we cannot assume that it has been deduced from Philippians 3⁵. C. G. Montefiore (*Judaism and St Paul* [London, 1914], p. 90) also calls in question Paul's stay in Jerusalem; against this see W. D. Davies, *St Paul and Rabbinic Judaism* (London, 1948), p. 2.

[2] See Feine–Behm, *Einleitung in das Neue Testament*, pp. 86 ff, and other works on 'problems of introduction'.

[3] Cf. H. J. Cadbury, K. Lake, F. J. Foakes Jackson, 'The Greek and Jewish Traditions of writing History', in *The Beginnings of Christianity*, II.7 ff, especially p. 15: 'In Acts the elaborate, homogeneous and schematic speeches suggest, if not the rhetoric, at least the free composition of the speeches in Greek and Roman histories.' See also Dibelius, '*Die Reden der Apostelgeschichte und die antike Geschichtsschreibung*', in *Aufsätze zun Apostelgeschichte* (Göttingen, 1951), pp. 120 ff.

[4] H. Bolkestein, '*De houding van den Romeinschen staat tegenover nieuwe en uitheemsche godsdiensten in den tijd der Republiek*', in *Mededeelingen der Nederlandsche Akademie van Wetenschappen*, Literature Section, New Series, Pt. IV.2.(Amsterdam, 1941).22.

[5] This also against G. Bornkamm who in his recent article '*Paulus*', in *Die Religion in Geschichte und Gegenwart* ([3rd edn, Tübingen, 1961], Vol. V, cols. 167–8), says that Paul grew up in Tarsus. Acts 22³ could, he says, betray a tendency to set Paul in a very close contact with Jerusalem from the outset; he seems to be very suspicious about ἀνατεθραμμένος ('according to 22³ he ought "to have grown up" there'), but accepts the fact that he had lived there for some time.

of Acts was a travelling companion of the apostle — and I see
no reason to doubt that — he very probably had good information at his disposal about Paul's history, and this is the more
likely since the details he gives cannot have been derived from
the epistles. After consideration of all sorts of possibilities, it is
not clear to me on the ground of what *texts* anyone would be
prepared to nullify the clear statement of Acts 22³ and 26⁴⁻⁵. I
shall have something to say presently about the general views
expressed in Paul's epistles and the impressions made by them
from which it is deduced that he must have had, as a mark of
his culture, so great an acquaintance with Greek and Hellenism
that he can have acquired it only in the years of his childhood
in Tarsus. Such arguments are entirely inconclusive.

As a counter argument, it cannot be put forward, as it is by
Findlay and Böhlig,[1] that on the interpretation given here
Paul must have known Jesus. According to them that is quite
impossible. But is that so certain? The answer to this question
is especially bound up with the interpretation of 2 Corinthians
5¹⁶, a verse from which completely opposite conclusions have
been drawn; according to some Paul says there that he did
indeed know Jesus in the time of His earthly life, according to
others that he never saw Him.[2] It seems to me unlawful pro-
cedure to turn down with the help of a doubtful text of this
kind a statement which in itself is as clear as crystal. One
ought rather to argue that Acts 22³ provides support for the
view that in 2 Corinthians 5¹⁶ Paul does in fact allude to an
acquaintance with Jesus in the time of His earthly life.

If then we may safely assume that in matters of fact Luke's
report is correct and that Paul had his early upbringing and his
education in Jerusalem, there arises the question, with which
we shall grapple in conclusion: *What approaches does this open
up for Pauline research?* I may be permitted to indicate briefly
a few points.

[1] G. G. Findlay, 'Paul the Apostle', in J. Hastings, *Dictionary of the
Bible* (Edinburgh, 1900), III.698b; Böhlig, *Die Geisteskultur von Tarsos
im augusteischen Zeitalter*, p. 152.
[2] Cf. H. Windisch, *Der zweite Korintherbrief* (9th edn, Göttingen,
1924), in loc.

In the first place, then, it must be taken as settled that all the fine dissertations about Paul's youth in Tarsus, about the experiences that he may have had there and what he took away from there as indelible youthful impressions, dissertations which at present usually constitute the opening chapter of his biography, must be relegated to the realm of fable. The texts have not been read correctly, and something has been smuggled into them.

In the second place, in biographies of the apostle all emphasis ought to fall on the fact that he grew up in the centre of Judaism, where the Torah prevailed in the home and in the street and determined both thought and action, in a strictly Pharisaic-religious environment, and that he, as it were, imbibed that atmosphere. He grew up not as a typical Jew of the Diaspora cut off from all that — it was as such a Jew that Klausner wanted to portray and explain him[1] — but as a man for whom there was only one possibility, one ideal and one delight, namely the fulfilment of the law and will of the Lord.

It is also implied — here is the third approach — that the tongue in which Paul learned to express himself in the days of his youth was not Greek but Aramaic. That he was bilingual is indeed assumed,[2] but in general we fail to see that this is taken seriously into account. It is of importance to be able to determine that Aramaic was the tongue in the use of which he was brought up, and that he did not as a child use Aramaic merely in his parental home and Greek in the world outside it — as is supposed by those who assume a long-continued stay in Tarsus — but that Aramaic was also the tongue spoken on the street and in school. It may be that people in Jerusalem also learned and spoke a little Greek (it has been assumed that this was so among the members of the groups which are mentioned

---

[1] *From Jesus to Paul* (London, 1946), is entirely constructed on this theme.

[2] On the strength of Philippians 3⁵ 'a Hebrew born of Hebrews'; see, e.g., Deissmann, *Paulus*, pp. 71–2; Windisch, *Der zweite Korintherbrief*, p. 351; M. Meinertz, *Einleitung in das Neue Testament* (5th edn, Paderborn, 1950), p. 70; A. Wikenhauser, *Die Apostelgeschichte und ihr Geschichtswert* (Münster i. W., 1921), p. 177.

in Acts 6[9] [see p. 49 above], and which may therefore be
compared to the Walloon Reformed Congregations in Hol-
land);[(1)] but Greek was to them a foreign language and Aramaic
was their own. Here we may let this complicated problem
rest.[(2)] But it can safely be said that Aramaic was his earliest
and principal tongue. It is my conviction that his epistles
testify that he thought in this tongue even when he expressed
his thoughts in Greek.[(3)] In any case it will no longer be possible to start investigations about the tongue which the apostle
used with the statement that he learned Greek from the
beginning and also a little Aramaic. Instead, serious account
will have to be taken of the fact that the development proceeded
the other way round. It is not sufficient to register only
elements of Hellenistic speech and style that are found in his
epistles; one must also take other factors into account. Moreover his epistles date from the last period of his life after he had
already spent some decades in a Greek environment, and he
had Greek collaborators.

Finally, as the fourth and most important approach, we may
consider what significance the result of our investigation has
for the weighty theme, Paul and Hellenism. One of the principal elements in the discussion of his youth in Tarsus has been
the acquaintance which he exhibits with the Greek tongue and
culture, and his sovereign command of the Septuagint. The
use which is made of this element is not always the same;

[1] In particular S. Greydanus (*Het gebruik van het Grieksch door den
Heere en Zijne Apostelen in Palestina* [Kampen, 1932]), has laid much
stress on the bilingual condition of Jerusalem and Palestine. But the
material collected by him and his evaluation of it, which cannot be discussed here, cannot possibly explain away the fact that Aramaic was
the spoken tongue of the land (cf. Josephus, p. 8, note 4 above). See
also H. Windisch, *Ἕλλην*, in Kittel, *Theologisches Wörterbuch zum
Neuen Testament*, II.508–9.
[2] Especially in its relation to the question whether Paul belonged to
a Cilician synagogue, as we assumed on p. 49 above.
[3] See my articles, '*Aramaeismen bij Paulus*', in *Vox Theologica*,
XIV.(1943).117–26; '*Reisepläne und Amen-sagen, Zusammenhang und
Gedankenfolge in 2 Korinthen* I[15–24]', in: *Studia Paulina in honorem
Johannis de Zwann* (Haarlem, 1953), pp. 215 ff; 'With unveiled face,
the exegesis of 2 Corinthians 3[12 ff]', in *Novum Testamentum*, V.(1961).

sometimes it is a matter that is *explained* by his childhood years
in Tarsus, and sometimes it functions as an *argument* ('where
would Paul have managed to acquire this knowledge if he had
not done so in Tarsus before his fifteenth year?'). It is thus
made to appear as if the later apostle had only once in his life
had a chance of coming into touch with Hellenism, namely in
his youth. It does not seem to be realized that this assumption
shows that one has already become the victim of a false
historical picture — a picture which is not less false because it
seems to be furthered by the peculiar composition of Acts or
because at present it is generally accepted. For — and here we
turn back to some observations which we made at the beginning, and set our subject in the great framework of Paul's life
— no account at all is taken of the fact that there was a period
of at least ten years after his conversion (our second period,
pp. 1–2) of which little or nothing is known, but which cannot
for that reason have been of small importance. For the most part
Paul spent this time in Tarsus, Cilicia, and Antioch. At that
time he had ample opportunity for contact with Hellenistic
culture in all its forms.[1] If we see contact at that time, full
justice is then done to Acts 22³ and to the Greek component in
Paul.

Perhaps there now arises the question: Strictly speaking,
does it matter much whether Paul was first in Jerusalem and
thereafter in Tarsus, or, as is generally believed, was in these
places the other way round? It certainly matters a great deal.
In the first place the question has been raised from which of
these cities Paul received his earliest impressions, and in view
of the great difference that there was in their manner of life
(see pp. 3–4 above) a right conclusion about the order that was
followed is here of significance. But in the second place it
follows, and is of outstanding significance, that according to
our representation of events Paul's main knowledge of Hellenism was gathered in his second period, that is to say *after
his conversion*, and thus from the beginning it was seen in the

---

[1] For the rest, the fact is not overlooked that Paul built up his
theology on the basis of Judaism.

light of the revelation in Christ. It makes a radical difference whether he was, as it were, drenched through with Hellenism *unconsciously* in his early years, as (contrary to Acts 22 and 26) is most often suggested, or *consciously* learned to see it first with the eyes of a Jew learned in the law and after that with the eyes of a Christian.

To put the problem of Paul's contact with Hellenism on the map of his youth in Tarsus is impossible. Historically, psychologically and theologically, this problem should in my opinion be handled with much more delicacy than it is treated at present. In this study I have tried to determine more clearly an important factor connected with it. I hope that in doing so I have made a contribution to the solution of this problem.

Appendix I

THE USE OF τρέφω
AND ITS DERIVATIVES
IN CONNECTION WITH UPBRINGING

IT IS EVIDENT that for a correct explanation of the triad found in Acts 22³ and elsewhere (see pp. 19 ff) a closer investigation is needed of the conceptual content of the word τρέφω and its derivatives. In particular, the sphere covered by this word must be accurately defined over against that covered by παιδεύω and its derivatives. Until now we have lacked an exact terminological analysis of the words which in the Greek tongue were used to describe upbringing in the widest sense. A few points may be found scattered here and there in the well-known work of Marrou and in the recent, more restricted study of Jentsch;[1] but these writers address themselves more particularly to *paideia* and do not discuss the synonyms of the Greek terminology of upbringing. Nor do the lexicons of Passow–Pape and Liddell–Scott give any further help. Kittel's *Theologisches Wörterbuch zum Neuen Testament* (9th edn) has not dealt with the question.[2] Within the limits of this study we can only point to the existence of this lacuna; the investigation which it necessitates cannot be made here. But it seems to me necessary to give very summarily and on the basis of a number of texts an analysis of the concept (ἀνα)τρέφω.

From a comparison of the passages given on pp. 19 ff it is at once clear that the simple τρέφω and the composite ἀνατρέφω were used as synonyms.[3] Alongside of them ἐκτρέφω may

---

[1] H. I. Marrou, *Histoire de l'éducation dans l'antiquité* (Paris, 1948), (the best general outline of the subject); W. Jentsch, *Urchristliches Erziehungsdenken* (Gütersloh, 1951), (especially on the notion 'paideia'). Further literature may be found listed in these books and in the dissertation of Boulogne (see p. 24, note 1).

[2] G. Bertram, 'παιδεύω', in G. Kittel–G. Friedrich, *Theologisches Wörterbuch*, VI.569 ff.

[3] See also Heliodorus, *Aethiopica*, X.13.7, θρέψας, and X.14.1, ἀναθρέψας.

E

also be named. It is not clear how far differences existed between these words in the living idiom or why one writer has a preference for one word and another for another (the LXX, e.g., has a strong preference for ἐκτρέφω), but this matter must here be left without further discussion. In any case the differences were not very great. That can be seen from a comparison of a few passages from the LXX with the renderings of them in Josephus.

JOSEPHUS, *Ant. Jud.*, VII.149 — paraphrase of Nathan's parable of the poor man's lamb: ταύτην μετὰ τῶν τέκνων αὐτὸς ἀνέτρεφε = 2 Samuel 12³ (LXX): ἐξέθρεψεν.

Ant. Jud., VIII.201: ἐξ ἧς υἱὸς αὐτῷ γενόμενος τοῖς τοῦ βασιλέως παισὶ συνανετράφη = 1 Kings 11²⁰ (LXX): καὶ ἐξέθρεψεν αὐτὸν Θεκεμίνα ἐν μέσῳ υἱῶν Φαραώ.

Ant. Jud., VIII.216: καλέσας δὲ τὰ μειράκια τὰ συντεθραμμένα = 1 Kings 12⁸ (LXX): καὶ συνεβουλεύσατο μετὰ τῶν παιδαρίων τῶν ἐκτραφέντων μετ' αὐτοῦ.

Ant. Jud., IX.125: παίδων ἑβδομήκοντα, τρεφομένων δ' ἐν Σαμαρείᾳ = 2 Kings 10⁶ (LXX): ἐξέτρεφον.

Ought it to be concluded from this that Josephus gave a paraphrase merely because a Greek writer of history had to render his sources not literally but in his own words,[1] or was ἀνατρέφω to his mind a more attractive word?

Whatever the answer to this question, it is clear that in respect of substance there was absolutely no difference between the words. The simple verb was the more used in the old tongue; ἀνατρέφω is one of the composites which later Greek preferred to it.[2]

---

[1] See on this H. J. Cadbury–K. Lake–F. J. Foakes Jackson in their contribution cited on p. 53, note 3.

[2] Cf. Blass–Debrunner, *Neut. Grammatik*, §116.1: 'The Koine prefers the compound verb where the classical speech can make-do with the simple one', and there ἀνατρέφω is given as an instance. According to J. H. Moulton–W. F. Howard (*A Grammar of New Testament Greek* [Edinburgh, 1929], II.296) we can in this case as in various other compounds perceive in the ἀνα 'a distinctly perfective force': 'to bring up'.

As our investigation relates to the ἀνατρέφω of men, passages which treat of plants and animals are not included in our discussion.

Texts in which τρέφειν and words connected with it stand for 'physical feeding', 'nutriment', and so on, are also left out of consideration. We consider that in the preliminary investigation initiated here we are entitled to make such a limitation. Nevertheless account ought constantly to be taken of the fact that this physical, we may almost say 'vegetative', conception is and remains firmly bound up with the notion. In the later Greek this original meaning did not fade away as it has done, for example, in the English word 'education', which in the seventeenth century meant the process of nourishing or rearing.

The (ἀνα)τροφή takes place *in the parental home* through mother and father.

PLATO, *Pol.*, IX.572.C — 'The history of his origin was, I believe, that he had been trained up (τεθραμμένος) from early years under the eye of a parsimonious father.'

PLATO, *Pol.*, V.449.D — in connection with the joint possession of women and children the question arises: πῶς θρέψουσι.

DEMOSTHENES, *In Nicostratum*, 1252 *ad fin.* — 'For she brought up (ἐξεθρέψατο) Cerdon from the time he was a small boy.'

PLUTARCH, *Pyrrhus*, 9.(388.A) — 'And all being skilled in arms, he brought them up (ἐθρέψατο) . . . even from their birth. . . .'

PLUTARCH, *Tib. Gracchus*, 8.(827.D) — the poor, expelled from the land, no longer enlisted 'or attended to the upbringing (ἀνατροφῆς) of their children'.

EPICTETUS, *Diss.*, III.22.68 — in a city of wise men cynicism is not necessary: the wise man marries 'for his wife will be another person like himself . . . and his children will be brought up (ἀνατραφήσεται) in the same fashion'.

PHILO, *Vita Mosis*, I.§II, see p. 36 above; it is striking that

E2

both parents say ἀνεθρέψαμεν, whilst of the mother γαλακτοτ-
ροφεῖν is used; in Josephus (see p. 39) the daughter of
Pharaoh, who assumes the role of the parents, also says
ἀναθρεψαμένη.

PAUL, Ephesians 6⁴ — among rules of conduct for fathers
in their dealings with their children: ἐκτρέφετε αὐτὰ ἐν παιδείᾳ
καὶ νουθεσίᾳ κυρίου.[1]

HERMAS, *Pastor, Visio*, III.9.1 — an address to children: 'I
brought you up (ἐξέθρεψα) in much simplicity and guileless-
ness.'

JUSTIN MARTYR, *Apol.*, 29.1 — Christians marry ἐπὶ παίδων
ἀνατροφῇ.

PORPHYRY, *ad Marcellam*, 1 — 'and your own children, if
one day, when we have brought them up (ὑφ' ἡμῖν ἀνατρε-
φόμενα), they apprehend the true philosophy.'

ORIGEN, *c. Celsum*, I.47 — James is the brother of Jesus 'not
so much on account of their relationship by blood, or of their
being brought up (ἀνατροφήν) together, as because of his
virtue and doctrine'.

The basis of this is the purely physical tie, the fact that 'nutrition' is a child's first need. This outward meaning of the word
continues for the time being to predominate, although, as
will appear later, it is not the only one. Because this is the
aspect that preponderates, the word can also be used of the
maintenance of slaves, to whose lot assuredly the real *paideia*,
which belonged to freemen, could not fall.

PLATO, *Leg.*, X.887.D — of little stories 'which they have
heard as babes and sucklings (ἐν γάλαξι τρεφόμενοι) from their
mothers and nurses'.

---

[1] Jentsch (*Urchristliches Erziehungsdenken*, p. 26) wrongly connects
this passage with texts from Plato where παιδεύω and τρέφω appear
alongside one another. The connecting of ἐκτρέφω with παιδεία
clearly indicates that the second word must here have the same
meaning as it has in the LXX, namely 'discipline'; where in classical
Greek the two notions appear side by side, they stand, as will be seen,
on quite different levels and παιδεία has always 'intellectual culture'
in view.

PLUTARCH, *Pericles*, 24.(165.C) — concerning Aspasia 'bringing up (τρέφουσαν) slave girls as prostitutes'.

PLUTARCH, *Phocion*, 38.(759.B) — 'and was in love with a slave girl who was being brought up (τρεφομένης) in the house of a brothel-keeper'.

HERMAS, *Visio*, I.1.1 — 'He who reared (θρέψας) me had sold me to one Rhoda in Rome.'

For other passages referring to slaves, see Liddell–Scott, *A Greek-English Lexicon*, Vol. II, s.v.

From the association of 'cattle' and 'slaves' in Liddell–Scott, it may be deduced that these were put on the same footing. In theory and practice this may often have been done. As regards τρέφω, the fact is not to be overlooked that Josephus uses this word of Samuel who as a boy dwelt with Eli (*Ant. Jud.*, V. 347: 'So Samuel dwelt and was brought up (τρεφόμενος) in the temple'), and of princes who moved in foreign court-circles (*Ant. Jud.*, XIX.360: 'At this time Agrippa was being brought up (τρεφόμενος) with Claudius Caesar' — he was 17 years of age, §354; XX.64: τέθραπτο γὰρ ὑπ' αὐτοῦ).

See also the passages from Appian cited on p. 71 below. Τρέφομαι then acquires the meaning 'to have one's abode'. But here also it refers to the sphere of the home. We can thus distinguish the nuances: to feed, to provide food and shelter, to allow to live in the family.

It follows that the τρέφειν in the most literal sense of the word fell at the outset to the charge of the mother or foster-mother; later it passed over to the father and became his care (or he passed it on to a 'pedagogue').[1] The special duty of the latter was to teach reading, γράμματα[2] as it was called. This τροφή was not limited to feeding. Those who in this period busied themselves with the child brought him forward in all sorts of ways to the point where the philosopher's task began.

---

[1] See Boulogne, *De plaats van de paedogogus in de Romeinse cultuur*, p. 31.

[2] On γράμματα see Schürer, *Geschichte des jüdischen Volkes im Zeitalter Jesu Christi*, p. 492, note 18.

PLATO, *Leg.*, X.887.D — see above, p. 62.

DEMOSTHENES, *In Aeschinem*, 249 — 'The mother ... brought up these many, whilst the father taught them reading.'

LUCIAN, *Anach.*, 20.(2.901) — Solon gives his vision of the nature of the state. In it upbringing plays a large part; 'their early breeding (ἀνατροφήν) we leave to their mothers, nurses and tutors, who are to rear them in the elements of a liberal education.'[1]

Cf. also his *Pseudol.*, 18.(3.176) — it avails nothing to pass yourself off as other than you are: the citizens of your own city ἴσασιν ἐκεῖνοι τὰς πρώτας σου τροφάς.

PLUTARCH, *Quomodo adolescens*, 14 — see p. 27 above.

According to QUINTILIAN, *Inst. Orat.*, I.1.16, Chrysippus would have wished the change-over to take place in the third year (see also p. 39 above): 'nevertheless he held the formation of the child's mind on the best principles to be a part of their duties'; but Quintilian himself (§15) held that the teaching of reading should not be delayed to the seventh year.

This continues until the child has reached an age of some understanding, and then he is handed over to teachers whose care is the real παιδεία.

PLATO, *Menex.*, 238.B — concerning the land — 'And when she had herself nursed (θρεψαμένη) them and brought them up to manhood, she gave them gods to be their rulers and teachers (διδασκάλους).'

PHILO, see p. 37 above.

LUCIAN, *Abdic.*, 9.(2.167): τοῖς ὅτε ἠγνόουν ἀναθρεψαμένοις — the ἀνατροφή thus refers to the period of ἄγνοια.

CLEMENT OF ALEXANDRIA, *Paed.*, III.12.97.3: 'But it is not my province, says the Instructor, to teach these any longer. But we need a Teacher of the exposition of these sacred words, to whom we must direct our steps. And now, in truth, it is time for me to cease from my instruction, and for you to listen

---

[1] Trans. of H. W. Fowler and F. G. Fowler.

to the Teacher. And He, receiving you who have been trained in excellent discipline (ὑπὸ καλῇ τεθραμμένους ἀγωγῇ), will teach (ἐκδιδάξεται) you the oracles.'[1] The fact that Clement applies this spiritually detracts nothing from the illustrative character of this passage.

Cf. *Paed.*, III.12.87.1: 'What has to be observed at home, and how our life is to be regulated, the Instructor (ὁ παιδαγωγός) has abundantly declared. And the things which He is wont to say to children by the way, while He conducts them to the Master (τὸν διδάσκαλον), these he suggests.'[1]

QUINTILIAN, *Inst. Or.*, I.2.1: 'but the time has come for the boy to grow up little by little, to leave the nursery, and tackle his studies in good earnest',[2] after which in §§2–4 the '*praeceptores*' are discussed.

This change-over probably took place at the age of seven, see Ps. PLATO, *Axiochus*, 366.D — every period of life has its own troubles; first the under-age child is discussed; then 'when he reaches the age of seven years, he endures many toils; pedagogues, schoolmasters, and gymnastic masters are appointed who govern him absolutely, and, as he grows up, critics, geometricians, and tacticians, a great multitude of despots'.

What the child learns at home has reference to tongue, customs, the formation of character, the most elementary laws of life, and this all comes under the notion ἀνατροφή (cf. also p. 69 below).

PLATO, *Protagoras*, 341.C — 'brought up (τεθραμμένος) in a foreign tongue.'

Cf. also *Apol.*, 18.A — 'if I speak in the language and manner in which I was brought up (ἐτεθράμμην).'

Leg., I.625.A — 'as you have been trained (τέθραφθε) in these institutions.'

Pol., IX.572.D — concerning a weakling: 'Well then . . .

---

[1] *Ante-Nicene Christian Library* trans.
[2] *Loeb Library* trans.

figure to yourself that this man has grown old in his turn, and that a young son is being bred up (τεθραμμένον) again in his habits.'

ARISTOTLE, *Eth. Nicom.*, X.ix.11 — 'He who is to be good must be brought up (τραφῆναι) and trained well.'

ARISTOTLE, *Pol.*, VII.6 — ἐν ἄλλοις τεθραμμένοι νόμοις.

PHILO — see p. 37 above.

JOSEPHUS, *c. Apionem*, I.269 — 'nor would they love laws quite contrary to those of their own country, and to those in which they had been bred up (ἐνετράφησαν) themselves.'

QUINTILIAN, *Inst. Or.*, I.i.9 — 'Their misconduct (that of the pedagogues) is no less prejudicial to morals. We are, for instance, told . . . that Leonides, Alexander's *paedagogus*, infected his pupil with certain faults, which as a result of his education as a boy clung to him even in his maturer years when he had become the greatest of kings.'[1]

QUINTILIAN, *Inst. Or.*, I.i.17 — 'Why, again, since children are capable of moral training, should they not be capable of literary education?'

PLUTARCH, *Comp. Gracch. c. Ag. et Cleom.* — see p. 22 above.

JUSTIN MARTYR, *Apol.*, 61.10 — after he has spoken about birth, Justin says: 'We were brought up in bad habits and wicked training (ἀνατροφαῖς).'

Dial. c. Tryph., 93 — 'and being debased by upbringing (ἀνατροφῆς), by wicked customs, and by sinful institutions, they lost their natural ideas.'

EUSEBIUS, *Praeparatio Evangelica*, IV.2.13: 'in whom what I most admire is how, after being brought up (τραφέντες) in the customs of the Greeks, and being taught even from the cradle, son from father, that those of whom we speak are gods, they have not been easily caught.'

That is why it is of such importance that, as parents for instance, people should conduct themselves well, and why the utmost care ought to be taken in selecting the foster-mothers

---

[1] *Loeb Library* trans.

and 'pedagogues' to whom the work is entrusted (in connection with this, the above-mentioned tracts of Plutarch, *de liberis educandis*, and Quintilian are of special importance). It was here assuredly in the circle of the home that the foundation was laid, and Plato has voiced the common mind in the words: 'The most important part of education (παιδείας) is right training in the nursery (τροφήν)' (*Leg.*, I.643.C).

The (ἀνα)τροφή *is thus that portion of a child's development which takes place in the sphere of the home, and which ought to instil into him a knowledge of the elementary laws of conduct in life and attitude to it.* After it — sometimes in the seventh year — there took place the change-over to typical instruction, when strangers began to act as teachers (the teaching of Socrates, see pp. 30–1 above, that the τροφή and the παιδεία should rest with one person is exceptional and has its origin in the fact that he himself was a philosopher). In its main features, probably with necessary variations in details, this schema remained the same throughout antiquity. [1]

It is thus clearly evident that the (ἀνα)τροφή *has a physical and a spiritual aspect, and these two sides of it belong together.* There is no reason at all to make such a division as we come across in Bauer (see p. 30 above); on the contrary, to do so would indeed mutilate the remarkable character of this notion.

This also holds good for a few passages from the Jewish Hellenistic literature which are mentioned in Bauer. Besides those that have already been discussed on pages 36 ff there may be noted:

Wisdom 7⁴ describes birth, which is the same for all men: 'in swaddling clothes was I nursed (ἀνετράφην) and with watchful care.'

---

[1] Cf. Marrou, *Histoire de l'éducation dans l'antiquité*, p. 200: 'Education properly so called, παιδεία never begins until seven years have gone past, the age at which the child is sent to school. Up to that time it is entirely a question of upbringing, (ἀνα)τροφή; but as appears in the present appendix there is something more to be said. For the Roman world see Boulogne, *De plaats van de paedogogus in de Romeinse cultuur*, *passim*.

(Cf. PHILO, *Leg. ad Gaium*, see p. 42 above.)

2 Maccabees 6²³ — Eleazer refused to dissemble, expressing an opinion which became his age and his 'conspicuous life as a citizen and his excellent upbringing (ἀνατροφῆς; but some MSS read ἀναστροφῆς, manner of life) from a child, or rather the holy laws of God's ordaining'.

4 Maccabees, 10² — Under tortures the second son cried: 'Know ye not that the same father begat me and my brothers that have died, and the same mother bore us, and in the same beliefs was I nurtured (ἀνετράφην)?'[1] The reference in this last clause is to the rules for the conduct of the Jewish life which were communicated to children from their earliest youth (cf. 9¹ — 'for we are ready to die rather than transgress the commands of our fathers').

4 Maccabees 11¹⁵ — The youngest son says: 'Being born and brought up (τραφέντες) for the same end, we should also die in like manner for the same cause.'

4 Maccabees 16⁸ — Lament of the mother whose seven sons have been brought to death: her pregnancies have been senseless, and to her sorrow has she given suck (16⁷). 'In vain did I endure for you, my sons, my many pangs, and the still more anxious cares of your upbringing (ἀνατροφῆς)'; whereupon she proceeds to speak about their adolescence.

JOSEPHUS, *Ant. Jud.*, IX.142 — Rescue of the later king Jehoash by his aunt: 'Finding Jehoash . . . who was not above a year old, concealed with his nurse, and taking him with her into the storeroom for the beds, she shut him up there, and she and her husband brought him up (ἀνέθρεψαν) privately . . . six years.'

Le livre de la prière d'Asenath (2nd edn), *Studia Patristica*, ed. P. Batiffol, I.(Paris, 1889)41: 'Now Asenath's large apartment, in which (till her eighteenth year) her maidenhood continued to be fostered (ἐτρέφετο), had three windows.'

The meaning of (ἀνα)τροφή which we have sketched above receives yet sharper definition when we consider a number of

---

[1] Trans. of C. W. Emmet.

passages in which the notion is found alongside that of παιδεία. For in addition to the very striking instances discussed on pp. 19 ff, there are others in which these notions are met with repeatedly alongside and as contrasts to one another.

As early as in Plato a few passages are met with which throw light on the contrast. In *Pol.*, VII.534.D he writes: Children of marriageable age should not be allowed, 'and certainly, if you ever had the actual training of these children of yours, whose training and education you are theoretically superintending, I cannot suppose that you would allow them to be magistrates in the State with authority to decide the weightiest matters, while they are as irrational (ἀλόγους) as the strokes of a pen'; cf. Plutarch, *Eumenes*, I: although Eumenes was of low origin, τραφῆναι δὲ ἐλευθερίως ἐν γράμμασι. Here the difference is clearly apparent: if the παιδεία is lacking, the children are still ἄλογοι even although they know the letters. In *Leg.*, IX.854.E, where there is discussion as to whether offences against the highest and most elementary commands to respect the gods, parents, and the State should be reckoned as serious when committed by strangers as by citizens, it is determined that 'if any citizen is ever convicted of such an act — that is, of committing some great and infamous wrong against gods, parents, or State — the judge shall regard him as already incurable, reckoning that, in spite of all the training and nurture (παιδείας τε καὶ τροφῆς) he has had from infancy, he has not refrained from the worst iniquity'. [1] Here τροφή is certainly mentioned to accentuate the seriousness of the situation. Not the παιδεία alone but also the τροφή from childhood which precedes it ought to inculcate something different in citizens. The τροφή thus begins earlier and comprises spiritual guidance, namely the inculcating of the elementary rules of conduct. In *Prot.*, 327.D, where the relativity of all things is spoken about, it is said: 'In like manner I would have you consider that he who appears to you to be the worst (ἀδικώτατος) of those who have been brought up in a law-abiding society (ἐν ἐννόμοις ἀνθρώποις) would appear to be a just man and an artificer of

[1] *Loeb Library* trans.

justice if he were to be compared with men who had no education (παιδεία) or courts of justice.' The position then is this, that a man who is regarded as altogether unrighteous in a normal society — i.e. in a developed community such as was considered ideal not only by Plato but also by the culture of the time of the Caesars — nevertheless appears to the uncivilized to be righteous as compared with a savage, because he has been brought up among ἔννομοι ἄνθρωποι. Among barbarians there is of course τροφή but no παιδεία; the ἀδικώτατος from a normal society, where there is also παιδεία, certainly lacks the latter, but he has received such a dowry from the ἔννομοι ἄνθρωποι that he can appear δίκαιος in the abnormal circumstances. Here, then, τρέφω refers to the stage before that of the παιδεία, but appears to comprise more than mere feeding; it imparts a certain manner of life, a certain behaviour.

In this connection it may be observed that πεπαιδευμένος is usual for 'perfectly well-bred' (see instances in Liddell–Scott, *A Greek-English Lexicon*, II.1287, s.v.); there τεθραμμένος cannot be substituted for it since it always indicates a lower level, cf., e.g., Plutarch, *Caius Gracchus*, 8.(838.C): Livius Drusus 'a man who in birth and upbringing (τεθραμμένος) was not behind any of the Romans', and 19.(843.E), where Cornelia, who found 'how much goodness of disposition and noble birth and upbringing (τετράφθαι) help to secure for us freedom from grief', is contrasted with those who expected παιδεία alone to give it; *Cicero*, 48.(885.D) — when they came to murder Cicero they found 'a young man, whom Cicero had instructed (τεθραμμένον) in the liberal arts and sciences', who repaid this benefit with treachery.

From Isocrates, *Areopagiticus*, 41, it may be concluded on a first reading that here τρέφω and παιδεύω are parallel notions, but in the light of the foregoing this appears not to be so, and this passage is brought into sharper relief. For a right ordering of the State, so Isocrates argues, the law must be, not external, but ἐν ταῖς ψυχαῖς, for, so he proceeds, 'it is not by legislation, but by morals, that States are well directed, since men who are badly reared (κακῶς τεθραμμένους) will venture to transgress even laws which are drawn up with minute exactness, whereas those who are well brought up (καλῶς πεπαιδευμένους) will be willing to respect even a simple code.'[1] Those then who have received as dowry from their homes only a manner of behaviour snap their fingers at the written laws; those on the other hand whose upbringing has been completed through schooling do not consider themselves to be exalted above the laws by their παιδεία, but are willing to abide by the elementary ones. Here also a difference in level is clearly perceptible; τεθραμμένος covers a sphere other than that of πεπαιδευμένος, and consequently something different is to be expected.

Worthy of note also for a correct idea of the ἀνατροφή is a comparison of two clauses in Appian, *Historia Romana*, VIII.37: In an emergency Hannibal sends messengers for help to Massinissa 'reminding him of his early life (διατριβῆς) and education (παιδεύσεως) at Carthage', and later it is added in explanation that he 'had in fact been brought up (τεθραμμένος) and educated (πεπαιδευμένος) at Carthage'. Here then, ἀνατροφή stands, as also does διατριβή (his stay),[2] over against the intellectual culture, which he had also received in Carthage; cf. also VIII.79: 'the very ground on which he had been nurtured and educated (ἐτράφη καὶ ἐπαιδεύθη).'[3]

Finally, as an instance that sums everything up, reference may be made to a usage in Herodian, *Ab excessu divi Marci*, I.2.1, that is especially instructive. After it has been related that there were born to Marcus Aurelius several daughters and two sons, the following is said about these latter: 'The second died when quite young. . . . The one who survived, Commodus by name, the father brought up (ἀνεθρέψατο) with the utmost care, engaging at salaries that were by no means contemptible the most notable in learning among the nations to attend his son continually and educate (παιδεύοιεν) him.' From this more can be deduced than the meaning 'moral and

[1] *Loeb Library* trans.
[2] Liddell–Scott, *A Greek-English Lexicon*, Vol. I, s.v.
[3] See also Lucian, *Somnium*, 12, where Paideia says: 'Now Socrates himself, who had been trained to the art of statuary, as soon as he perceived what was better ran away from it and deserted to me.'

spiritual nurture, to educate', which is all that is deduced from it, for example, by Bauer (col. 127). From the distinction drawn between the sons, one of whom died in infancy, it appears that Marcus Aurelius surrounded the other who survived with great care; this care had of course reference to what was physical as well as to what was mental, and comprised the whole life of the child. Here again the ἀνατροφή is carried out by the father in the sphere of the home, the medium used, namely Marcus' personal exertions, being underlined (he did this himself and did not hand it over to 'pedagogues', as was all too customary in imperial times).[1] The παιδεύειν is clearly distinct from this: for it the help of strangers is called in. παιδεύειν refers then to school instruction, to typical intellectual culture.

The results of the foregoing investigation are gathered together on pp. 33 f above.

[1] On this see Marrou, *Histoire de l'éducation dans l'antiquité*, *passim*, and Jentsch, *Urchristliches Erziehungsdenken*, pp. 25 ff.

Appendix II

(see p. 5, note 2)

ALPHABETICAL LIST OF NAMES IN CHRONOLOGICAL BIBLIOGRAPHY

Aalders, G. J. D., 39
Adam, Karl, 42
Baljon, J. M. S., 3
Bauer, W., 23, 44
Beus, Ch. de, 40
Beyschlag, W., 1
Böhlig, H., 6
Brandon, S. G. F., 41
Brouwer, A. M., 22
Bultmann, R., 19
Clemen, C., 4
Deissmann, A., 13
Dibelius, M., 38
Dobschütz, E. von, 14
Enslin, M. S., 24
Fascher, E., 20
Findlay, G. G., 2
Glover, T. R., 25
Goguel, M., 29
Grossouw, W. K. M., 31
Hatch, W. H. P., 42, 43
Holzner, J., 32
Howard, W. F., 42
Imschoot, P. van, 26
Jülicher, A., 20
Klausner, J., 28
Knopf, R., 36

Kümmel, W. G., 38
Lietzmann, H., 36
Liechtenhahn, R., 35
Loewenich, W. von, 34
Meinertz, M., 37
Montefiore, G. C., 7
Nock, A. D., 27
Prat, F., 33
Puukko, A. F., 18
Rhijn, C. H. van, 1
Ricciotti, G., 30
Robinson, B. W., 15
Schoeps, H. J., 46
Sevenster, J. N., 40
Stalker, J., 10
Steinmann, A., 17
Unnik, W. C. van, 40
Veldhuizen, A. van, 9
Waszink, J. H., 40
Weinel, H., 36
Weiss, J., 8
Wikenhauser, A., 11, 45
Wilson, T., 16
Wrede, W., 5
Zwaan, J. de, 21
Zahn, Th., 12

CHRONOLOGICAL BIBLIOGRAPHY

1 W. Beyschlag–C. H. van Rhijn, *Paulus*, in E. Riehm–C. H. van Rhijn, *Bijbelsch Woordenboek* (Utrecht, 1894), Pt. II, pp. 338–41.

2 G. G. Findlay, 'Paul the Apostle', in J. Hastings, *Dictionary of the Bible* (Edinburgh, 1900), III.697–9.

3 J. M. S. Baljon, *Geschiedenis van de boeken des Nieuwen Verbonds* (Groningen, 1901), pp. 2–3.

4 C. Clemen, *Paulus, sein Leben und Wirken* (Giessen, 1904), II.60 ff.

5 W. Wrede, *Paulus* (Halle, 1904), pp. 5–7.

6 H. Böhlig, *Die Geisteskultur von Tarsus* (Göttingen, 1913), pp. 151–3.

7 G. C. Montefiore, *Judaism and St Paul* (London, 1914), p. 90.

8 J. Weiss, *Das Urchristentum* (Göttingen, 1917), pp. 131 ff.

9 A. van Veldhuizen, *Paulus en zijn brief aan de Romeinen* (2nd edn, Groningen–Den Haag, 1918), p. 5.

10 J. Stalker, 'Paul', in J. Hastings, *Dictionary of the Apostolic Church* (Edinburgh, 1918), II.144–5.

11 A. Wikenhauser, *Die Apostelgeschichte und ihr Geschichtswert* (Münster i.W., 1921), p. 177.

12 Th. Zahn, *Die Apostelgeschichte* (1st and 2nd edns, Erlangen–Leipzig, 1926), II.750–1 (giving earlier publications of his in which he has presented the same opinion).

13 A. Deissmann, *Paulus* (2nd edn, Tübingen, 1926), pp. 71–4.

14 E. von Dobschütz, *Der Apostel Paulus* (Halle [Saale], 1926), pp. 2–3.

15 B. W. Robinson, 'Influences leading toward the conversion of Paul', in *Festgabe für Adolf Deissmann* (Tübingen, 1927), p. 109.

16 T. Wilson, *St Paul and Paganism* (Edinburgh, 1927).

17 A. Steinmann, *Zum Werdegang des Paulus, die Jugendzeit in Tarsus* (Freiburg i.Br., 1928), (also his commentary, *Die Apostelgeschichte* [Bonn]).

18 A. F. Puukko, *Paulus und das Judentum* (Helsinki, 1928), pp. 11–23.

19 R. Bultmann, '*Paulus*', in *Religion in Geschichte und Gegenwart* (2nd edn, Tübingen, 1930), Vol. IV, cols. 1020–1.

20 A. Jülicher–E. Fascher, *Einleitung in das Neue Testament* (7th edn, Tübingen, 1931), pp. 33–4.

21 J. de Zwaan, *De Handelingen der Apostelen* (2nd edn, Groningen–Den Haag, 1931), p. 142 (cf. also his *Inleiding tot het Nieuwe Testament* [2nd edn, Haarlem, 1948], Pt. II, p. 14).

22 A. M. Brouwer, *Paulus de Apostel*, Pt. II, *De mensch en zijn tijd* (Zutphen, 1934), pp. 85–118.

23 W. Bauer, *Griechisch-deutsches Wörterbuch zu den Schriften des Neuen Testaments* (3rd edn, Berlin, 1937), col. 1062.

24 M. S. Enslin, *Christian Beginnings* (New York, 1938), p. 180.

25 T. R. Glover, *Paul of Tarsus* (4th edn, London, 1938), pp. 15–24.

26 P. van Imschoot, '*Paulus*', in *Bijbels Woordenboek* (Roermond z.j.), col. 1237.

27 A. D. Nock, *St Paul* (2nd edn, London, 1946), pp. 21–34.

28 J. Klausner, *From Jesus to Paul* (London, 1946), pp. 308–9.

29 M. Goguel, *La naissance du christianisme* (Paris, 1946), pp. 231–5.

30 G. Ricciotti, *Paolo Apostolo* (Rome, 1946), pp. 213–19.

31 W. K. M. Grossouw, *St Paulus en de beschaving van zijn tijd* (Nijmegen–Utrecht, 1947), pp. 4–5.

32 J. Holzner, *Paulus* (2nd edn, Voorhout, 1948), pp. 30 ff.

33 P. Pratt, *La théologie de St Paul* (38th edn, Paris, 1949), I.20.

34 W. von Loewenich, *Paulus, sein Leben und Werk* (Witten, 1949), pp. 31 ff.

35 R. Liechtenhahn, *Paulus, seine Welt und sein Werk* (2nd edn, Basel, o.J.), p. 35.

36 R. Knopf–H. Lietzmann–H. Weinel, *Einführung in das Neue Testament* (5th edn, Berlin, 1949), pp. 335–6.

37 M. Meinertz, *Einleitung in das Neue Testament* (5th edn, Paderborn, 1950), pp. 70–1 (Paul was 'already in his early youth . . . in Jerusalem', nevertheless it was Tarsus that urged him on to acquaint himself with Hellenism).

38 M. Dibelius–W. G. Kümmel, *Paulus* (Berlin, 1951), pp. 28–30.

39 G. J. D. Aalders, *Paulus en de antieke cultuurwereld* (Kampen, 1951), p. 17.

40 J. N. Sevenster, '*Paulus*', in J. H. Waszink–W. C. van

Unnik–Ch. de Beus, *Het Oudste Christendom en de antieke cultuur* (Haarlem, 1951), Pt. II, p. 262.

41 S. G. F. Brandon, *The Fall of Jerusalem and the Christian Church* (London, 1951), pp. 16, 62, 130.

42 *Paulus-Hellas-Oikumene* (*an ecumenical Symposium*) (Athens, 1951), with the articles by Karl Adam, W. H. P. Hatch and W. F. Howard referred to in note 3 on p. 5 above.

43 W. H. P. Hatch, 'The Life of Paul', in *The Interpreter's Bible* (Nashville, 1951), VII.190.

44 W. Bauer, *Griechisch-deutsches Wörterbuch zu den Schriften des Neuen Testaments* (5th edn, Berlin, 1958), col. 1263: 'Born ... in Tarsus, he certainly grew up there.'

45 A. Wikenhauser, *Einleitung in das Neue Testament* (Freiburg i.Br., 1953), p. 250 (Paul came to Jerusalem at the age of eighteen to twenty).

46 H. J. Schoeps, *Paulus, die Theologie des Apostels im Lichte der jüdischen Religionsgeschichte* (Tübingen, 1959), p. 5. He mentions the Dutch edition of the present study in a footnote, but does not discuss its argument; Paul came from Tarsus to Jerusalem as a νεανίας (Acts 7⁵⁷) when sixteen or seventeen years old.